D1799244

The Parents' Green Guide

The Parents' Green Guide

PROTECTING CHILDREN AND THE ENVIRONMENT

Brigid McConville

PANDORA

LONDON SYDNEY WELLINGTON

First published by Pandora Press, an imprint of the
Trade Division of Unwin Hyman Ltd, in 1990.
© Brigid McConville 1990.

Pandora Press
Unwin Hyman Limited
15/17 Broadwick Street
London W1V 1FP

Unwin Hyman Inc
8 Winchester Place, Winchester, MA 01890, USA

Allen & Unwin Australia Pty Ltd
PO Box 764, 8 Napier Street, North Sydney, NSW 2060, Australia

Allen & Unwin New Zealand Pty Ltd with the Port Nicholson Press
Compusales Building, 75 Ghuznee Street, Wellington, New Zealand

British Library Cataloguing in Publication Data
McConville, Brigid
    The parents' green guide : protecting children and their future.
    1. Children. Social development
    I. Title
    305.23

ISBN 0-04-440564-2

Typeset in Great Britain by Wyvern Typesetting Ltd
Printed in Great Britain by Cox & Wyman Ltd, Reading

For Maeve and Arthur

ABOUT THE AUTHOR

Brigid McConville is a freelance journalist and author. She was educated at Trinity College, Dublin and at Berkeley, University of California. In 1981 she was runner-up in the Catherine Pakenham Award for young women journalists, and is a contributor to *The Times*, *Guardian* and *Woman* magazine. She is the author of many short stories and her books include *Women Under the Influence: Alcohol and its Impact*, *Sisters* and *Mad to be a Mother* as well as several for children. She was the Editor of *Hinkley Inquirer* during the Inquiry into nuclear-power at Hinkley in Somerset and is one of the founders of the local magazine *Justwomen*. She lives in Somerset with her partner and two children.

Contents

Acknowledgements

Thanks to Friends of the Earth for their help, advice, and unstinting flow of information. Thanks also to the Women's Environmental Network for their Ideal Green Home Initiative and contributions to the great nappy debate. The London Food Commission, the National Trust, Damian Randle of *Green Teacher*, the organic gardening centre HDRA, and the Commonwork Centre have all been generous with their time and ideas.

My researcher Celia Richardson of the Green Chip environmental consultancy did sterling work in turning up enough information for a series of books.

At Pandora, my editors Candida Lacey and Ginny Iliff were a warm source of support and ideas as well as keen critics.

My friends Jill Sutcliffe, Gilly Lee, Danielle Grunberg and Faith Dethier, my sister Lucy and my parents Beryl and Mike McConville, all kept me primed with new ideas, observations and gleanings of information. And many thanks to Delia Collins for looking after Arthur.

Finally, especial thanks to my partner John who made me lunch and made me go for walks, and to our children Maeve and Arthur who are the reasons for all of it.

The Author and Publishers would like to thank the authors and publishers quoted in this book.

Introduction

It can be tough for parents these days. True, we generally don't have to worry about smallpox, the plague or starvation, but what about polluted food, water, air, land and seas? What about the destruction of the rainforests, the ozone layer and global warming?

As each day passes we are bombarded with more bad news about the risks to children from radioactivity or pesticide residues. Meat, fish, cheese, vegetables, bread, eggs, drinking, walking, swimming, watching telly – you name it, it's no longer healthy. And in the long term, what kind of a world will we be leaving to our children?

The danger, all of a sudden, is that with a mass groan of 'Oh no, the environment . . . !', parents everywhere will collapse into a deep apathy born of boredom with depressing news and a sense of their own powerlessness to change things.

This book sets out to counter that sense of powerlessness by showing that there are many simple, easy and enjoyable things that parents – and children – can do for a safer and greener future.

At home, the heart of life with children, we can make many small but significant changes, so that we consume differently, pollute less, and conserve more. For, as E.F. Schumacher of *Small is Beautiful* put it:

> 'We must do what we conceive to be the right thing and not bother our heads or burden our souls with whether we're going to be successful. Because if we don't do the right thing, we'll be doing the wrong thing, and we'll just be part of the disease and not a part of the cure.'

As for feeding our children (that most crucial and symbolic of parental activities), we can arm ourselves with the available facts, press for the unavailable ones and make choices. We can choose food that is safe, healthy and that does not involve cruelty or pollution in its manufacture.

Similarly we can take action to safeguard our children from polluted air and contaminated water, and we can take them out to enjoy the delights and richness of the land they live in. Very often, all we have to do is take our cue from our children who are arguably the most environmentally clued-up group in the whole community.

In our children's day-to-day lives, at home and at school, we can help them to develop a love for life, a respect for the Earth and a true confidence in their own worth. There are as many ways to do this as there are parents and children, and I hope that parents will be able to draw on this book as a source of ideas which can be reworked to suit themselves. (Certainly, the ideas described here are only the tip of the iceberg, and if it wasn't practically necessary to stop adding new snippets, the book could have gone on forever.)

Parents, perhaps more than any other group, dread what is being done to the environment. For most of us, the care and well-being of our children is central to our lives. It is what we care about more than anything else. Yet children – together with pregnant women – are amongst the most vulnerable to the hazards of pollution and contamination.

People everywhere are making it quite clear that they will not put up with the destruction of the environment any longer. Change is in the air. Groups of parents, of children, of young people are talking, taking action, recycling, preserving, planting, campaigning, cycling, choosing and refusing – while showing an unbounded enthusiasm for reclaiming their birthright, the Earth.

I hope *The Parents' Green Guide* will give parents some of the information they need to make this a safer, healthier, more beautiful world for our children.

For our children are the future.

1

Home

> 'In reality we all inhabit the same home, and there's only one of it.'
>
> John Button

HOME LIFE IN THE AGE OF WASTE

Home is at the heart of life with children. It is the environment that we create for them, to bring them up safely, in good health and happiness. It is also the place where they will learn the daily habits and attitudes which can affect their whole lives. And it is one small 'ecosystem' over which we can have some control.

If your children are old enough, it's quite likely that they are well ahead of you in terms of green consciousness. Far from parents having to educate their children in environmental concern, it's more often the other way around: children can see what we have been doing to their world, and many have taken the initiative in seeking change – starting with home life.

This is the Age of Waste, and none of us is innocent. Every time we switch on a light, start the car, go shopping or cook a meal we are involved in a long chain of consumption which ends up in some degree of pollution or exploitation of the planet. And the more sophisticated our lives become, the harder it is to unravel all the environmental costs of the way we live.

'When in the 1850s the German zoologist Ernst Haeckel was wondering what to call the new science of the study of living things within their environmental context, he chose the word *okologie*, which was rapidly taken into English as "ecology". The term derives from the Greek word *oikos* and *logos*, meaning "the study of homes". We may call the homes of plants and animals "habitats", but our own suburban semi, country cottage or city flat is just as much our habitat as the wood is the foxes' home or the mountaintop the eagle's.'

John Button in *Green Pages* (Optima).

Most of us take our energy supplies absolutely for granted. For light, we flick a switch. To cook, we turn a knob. To travel, we fill our cars with petrol. Most of this energy comes directly or indirectly from oil and coal. But these resources are finite – our children will not thank us for squandering them – and their use creates pollution.

The fumes from power-station chimneys and exhaust eventually falls as acid rain. Nuclear power seems cleaner, but it produces pollution on a scale that most of us don't begin to understand. Only disasters like Chernobyl can illustrate the potential destructive power of the nuclear option.

Our overuse of energy has been damaging the atmosphere in the greenhouse effect – mostly caused by a build-up of carbon dioxide from burning fossil fuels. As the atmosphere warms up, the sea level may rise to such an extent that it causes catastrophic flooding, threatening whole countries. (See Pollution.)

'The other way we use energy is when it's bound up in the highly processed goods we buy. A tin of beans might take only a minute or two and a very small amount of domestic power to heat up, but energy will already have been used to produce the fertilizer to grow the crop, to fuel the tractors, the harvesters and the delivery lorries. The canning process and manufacture of the cans will have used even more, and while the cans sit on the shelf in the shop, it will be using up electric lighting and heating.'

Chris Baines in *The Big E*.

ENERGY SAVING

Nearly a third of domestic energy is wasted because of poor insulation. In other words, much of the heat in our homes goes straight out through the walls and roofs into the outside world. And so people turn up their heating, put up fuel bills – and add to the greenhouse effect as power stations produce more carbon dioxide in making electricity.

One kilowatt of electricity buys you about two hours ironing, two hours vacuuming, one hour of one bar of a radiant electric heater, or three gallons of hot water. For every one kilowatt of electricity used, Britain's power industry emits 10·1 grams of sulphur dioxide into the air. This eventually falls as acid rain, damaging buildings, devastating forests, lakes and wildlife and affecting human health.

We have to keep energy use as low as possible if we want to minimize the greenhouse effect, and home insulation is a vital part of this strategy. There are a whole range of things you can do to save energy, from the most direct and simple in your own home to pressing for a change in national policy.

- Turn down your heating: *Mother and Baby* magazine recommend a house temperature of about 18°C, but many of us have brought up healthy children (or we ourselves have been brought up) at far brisker temperatures. True, newborn babies do need to be kept warm until their own 'thermostats' get going, but it should be possible to keep one room warm for the baby without keeping the whole house like an oven. And your family are more likely to avoid colds if they put on warm clothes and play in the fresh air than if they stay in a stale, centrally-heated atmosphere all day.

- As for hot water, there is no point in heating it up so much that it scalds your children when it comes out of the tap. It's also wasteful to bring it up to boiling point so that you have to add cold water to cool it down:

keep it at a comfortable temperature for hand washing – and make sure your immersion heater is well lagged.

- Use a shower rather than a bath to save heat and water.
- Keep saucepan lids on when you are cooking, and turn the heat down as low as possible.
- Don't put more water than you need into the kettle, and descale it regularly to help it boil faster.
- As soon as it gets dark, draw the curtains, thicker the better, over every window. In bigger, older houses, curtains can be used to block draughts around doorways and at strategic points in halls and corridors, too.
- Children are forever charging about the flat or the house and leaving doors open, so it's a good idea to fit automatic door-closing devices.
- Draughtproof your windows with the commercially made strips – or home-made equivalents (such as newspaper).
- Fit draughty doors with draught excluders, or bring back the old-fashioned fabric 'sausage' to lie at the foot of the door.
- Cavity insulation can reduce heat loss by a half.
- The government's Energy Efficiency Office has a range of free leaflets on home insulation, for details contact the Department of Energy, Thames Bank South, Millbank, London SW1T 4QJ. Your local council may run an energy advice centre, too.

MORE LIGHT THAN HEAT

The average electric light bulb wastes a vast amount of energy. But apart from turning them off, you can now save energy with energy-efficient light bulbs. These bulbs are an expensive investment compared to the standard variety (about £15 each, at time of writing), but they use 80 per cent less energy in the course of their life. And as they last for nearly one year of continuous use, they are cheaper in the long run. They are available from good lighting shops, or Wotan Lights Ltd, Wotan House, 1 Gresham Way, London SW19 8HU (tel: 081 947 1261).

HOME HEAT

Home heating and hot water account for some 80 per cent of domestic energy consumption. The Bristol Energy Centre – which specializes in domestic energy conservation and fuel poverty – has a demonstration house where you can see the best of energy-saving strategies in practice. Unfortunately, like many 'green' alternatives, the poorer you are the less likely you are to be able to afford energy conservation. If you want more information, contact the Bristol Energy Centre, 101 Philip Street, Bedminster, Bristol BS3 4DR (tel: 0272 662008).

But if you are starting from scratch with your heating system, the Women's Environmental Network recommends the gas condensor boiler which is at least 20 per cent more efficient than other comparable boilers. Their *Green Living* magazine, describing their 'Green Home' exhibition, gives details of stockists for a wide range of 'green' domestic products and appliances.

Some people find it hard to live with the fact that some 17 per cent of an electricity bill in Britain goes to pay for the electricity boards' use of nuclear energy. If you don't want to be part of this system, you should contact CANE – Consumers Against Nuclear Energy. They organize a campaign in which you withhold the nuclear proportion of your electricity bill and pay it into a CANE Trust account. Eventually, the money has to be paid to the various electricity boards, but in the meantime interest on the money is spent on research into renewable energy. Send a stamped addressed envelope to CANE, PO Box 697, London NW1 8YQ for details.

HOW WE SQUANDER OUR RESOURCES

- People now create more rubbish than ever before in history: up to ten times our body weight in textiles, paper, glass, plastic, metal and kitchen waste every year.
- Some four and a half billion drinks cans were chucked away in Britain in 1986. Placed end to end they would have reached the moon. Include aerosol cans and you could go to the moon and back again.
- The average British family of four threw away the equivalent of six trees' worth of paper in 1987.
- Five per cent of your shopping bill pays for packaging – which is mostly unnecessary and polluting.
- Each year 7·7 million tonnes of paper and board are used in Britain. Some five million tonnes of this are chucked away.
- When paper is made from waste rather than wood-pulp, only half as much energy is needed.
- Most of our rubbish currently goes into landfill sites: but by the end of the century we may have run out of places to put it.
- Europe's indigenous forests are being replaced by massive conifer plantations which eventually make the soil acidic and destroy plant and animal habitats.
- As tropical rainforests are cut down in Central America and Asia, eucalyptus trees are sometimes planted for paper production. But the eucalyptus soak

up so much water that they destroy the soil structure, eventually causing erosion and environmental damage.

RECYCLING THOSE RESOURCES

Doing something positive about the environment – like charity – begins at home.

Consider your dustbin. Is it a mish-mash of potato peelings and tin cans, glass bottles and paper, plastic packaging and 'disposable' nappies? This need not be so. Three-quarters of our household rubbish could be reused or recycled. Lots of packaging – boxes, toilet rolls, and empty cartons – can be saved for children to play with (see Play).

'Household waste is an indiscriminate mixture of a huge variety of things which ought never to have been thrown in the same waste bin in the first place. Once this mixture has been covered by earth, it starts to react with itself . . . Substances from the chemical part of the rubbish – mercury, cadmium and nickel from batteries, waste solvents, weed killers and the like – are washed through the soil to reappear as drinking water. Instead of being sealed, the tip becomes a fountainhead of pollution.'

John Seymour and Herbert Girardet in
Blueprint for a Green Planet
(Dorling Kindersley).

Nearly 30 per cent of our rubbish is paper and card which is excellent material for recycling. Glass too can be recycled, saving energy, cutting pollution and reducing the need for raw materials. Many local authorities and some supermarkets are now providing bottle banks, and some have collection points for recycling paper and cans. Contact the council or your area's Friends of the Earth branch will tell you about local facilities; their head office at 26–8 Underwood Street, London N1 7JQ (tel: 081 450 1555) has a recycling unit.

'The trouble [with plastics] is that they last forever, and although recycling is possible in theory it is a long way off in practice. Much packaging is made from layers of different plastics, which cannot be reprocessed in combination. There are also toxicity problems associated with many plastics, and dangerous dioxins are given off when they are incinerated.'

Karen Christensen in *Home Ecology* (Arlington Books).

The key is sorting and separating waste: instead of the one kitchen bin, you need several. First and foremost is the compost bucket. Anyone with the smallest garden can accumulate a rich compost heap from left-over food and vegetable peelings. It soon becomes a habit to put organic matter straight into the compost bucket, and it is deeply satisfying to see it rot down into a lovely pungent food for the soil as the months go by.

Secondly – depending on the recycling facilities in your

area – you will need a few boxes for your old glass bottles and jars, plus a box for paper and card. If you have a metal can recycling system nearby, so much the better: add a box for cans.

Once you become rubbish-conscious, you will take a strange pride in the lightness of your dustbin at the end of the week, and your priorities in shopping will gradually change with an eye to packaging. Paper packaging becomes preferable to plastic; glass bottles and jars will win over tins. You will see the advantages of buying in bulk, and carrying your own shopping bags rather than accepting plastic carriers.

RAGS AND BONES

Once you start to think about it, almost everything we throw away could be reused somehow – or at least disposed of more safely. Here are just some of the home items that could have a new lease of life before the rubbish tip:

- **Clothes and rags:** old textiles still have plenty of uses. Clothes and bedding in good condition can be reused: take them to jumble sales (local churches or community centres are always collecting jumble) or charity shops like Oxfam. Clothes that don't sell or get sent to Third World countries are sold to textile re-cycling factories. Mixed rags can be spun into new cloth, used as stuffing or made into industrial wipes. Oxfam makes about a million pounds a year in this way. Keep interesting clothes and shoes for the children's dressing-up box.
- **Spectacles:** a variety of groups collect old pairs of glasses which are sent out to Third World countries for reuse. Try your local Christian Aid or Oxfam branch.

- **Toys:** slightly damaged or unwanted toys can be used again by other children. Take them to charity shops, jumble sales, hospitals or to your local Children's Scrapstore which recycles toys and play materials for children's groups. Contact Children's Scrapstore, Federation of Resource Centres, Greater Manchester Play Resource Unit, Grumpy House, Vaughan Street, West Gorton, Manchester M12 5DU (tel: 061 223 9730) for details. (See Play.)
- **Books:** there are plenty of outlets for second-hand books: dealers, shops, jumble sales. Oxfam collect them for fundraising purposes.
- **Bric-a-brac:** odds and ends you don't really use may find a useful home with someone else – via charity shops and jumble sales, or very often as games for the children.
- **Magazines and comics:** don't throw them away; your local hospital or doctors' surgery may welcome them.
- **Medicine:** bottles containing old medicine can be returned to a chemist.
- **Motor Oil:** oil can easily be recycled for further use as heating or lubricating oil. Used sump oil is a serious pollutant and tipping it into the drains is an offence. Nor should it be poured onto the ground or burned in the open air. Ask Friends of the Earth about recycling facilities, or contact your local council.

Waste Not is a booklet from the Charities Aid Foundation which lists over 450 organisations and charities which collect 'waste', ranging from postage stamps to furniture, sports equipment to spectacles. It costs £2.95 (including postage and packing) from CAF, 48 Pembury Road, Tonbridge, Kent TN9 2JD.

RECYCLING CHILDREN

Many local voluntary groups are getting people involved
in recycling schemes, reclaiming thousands of tonnes of
unwanted materials. Waste Watch, based at the National
Council for Voluntary Organisations, promotes and supports these local initiatives. Children very much enjoy
getting involved in recycling too, gathering cans wherever
they can find them and chucking bottles into the bottle
bank. It's a habit that will set them up for life.

The children's club WATCH in Hampshire, which is
part of the Hampshire and Isle of Wight Naturalists'
Trust, have set up successful recycling schemes. They
appealed to people to save aluminium foil, cans and
saucepans and they got such a massive response that the
Trust set up a feasibility study which showed strong public
support for an aluminium recycling scheme, with a part-
time co-ordinator.

Send for the Waste Watch information pack *Recycling:
a practical guide for local groups*, which is published by
the Shell Better Britain Campaign, Red House, Red
House Park, Hill Lane, Great Barr, West Midlands B43
6LZ. You can also apply to the Shell Better Britain
Campaign for a grant of up to £500 to support recycling
work. The address of the National Council for Voluntary
Organisations is 26 Bedford Square, London WC1B 3HU
(tel: 071 636 4066), or ring your council for details of local
recycling schemes. WATCH Groups are run by local wildlife trusts (or trusts for nature conservation) under the
national umbrella of the RSNC (Royal Society for Nature
Conservation) c/o WATCH Trust, 22 The Green, Nettleham, Lincolnshire LN2 2NR (tel: 0522 752326).

An important part of Friends of the Earth's work is
promoting recycling in the community, and some good
examples are provided by their Avon branch which has a

Ideas from overseas

- According to the Danish authorities, 99 per cent of all beer and soft drinks bottles sold in Denmark are collected and refilled.

- In several towns in West Germany, houses have a green bin – for kitchen waste, paper and cardboard – and a grey bin, for non-organic rubbish. Contents of the green bins are sent to composting yards, the grey bins to the tip or incinerator.

- In Long Island, USA, Suffolk County has banned almost all non-biodegradable plastic packaging at retail establishments.

- In Switzerland, PVC in household waste has been cut by 60 per cent since industry signed a voluntary agreement with the Federal Office for Environmental Protection. PVC bottles were replaced with PET (easier to recycle), and packaging has become more environment friendly – more paper products, less plastic.

- In the 'blue bin' system which operates in Ontario, Canada, householders are supplied with a special bin for glass, cans and plastic bottles. They are asked to stack newspaper and textiles separately. Some 80 per cent of Ontario householders take part in the scheme and, as a result, over half their domestic waste is extracted for recycling. A new scheme in Sheffield in Britain, is following suit, providing 10,000 households with a plastic bin for their recyclable waste.

- West Germany has introduced a deposit on all plastic drink containers. From 1991, all packaging made from materials other than paper must be biodegradable.

variety of well-established schemes – including a team which works with children.

Their community education team visits schools and small groups in the area to involve children in recycling activities. Rag-rug weaving, poster and collage making, stories, talks and a large walkabout board game bring the subject alive for children; they are encouraged to try recycling their own paper by making it out of newspaper pulp; they also see the 'Once is not enough' video, in which Captain Cleanup and The Kid take a light-hearted look at recycling. Get in touch with the Avon Friends of the Earth, Arnos Castle Estate, Junction Road, Brislington. Bristol BS4 3JP (tel: 0272 715446).

NAPPIES: BACK TO THE BUCKET?

Every parent of young children will have strong views about nappies: after all, those years before children are potty trained can seem like one long nappy-changing marathon.

So-called disposables did seem to be the answer. No more scraping and washing and drying – just bundle them in the bin. What a liberating invention they were, indispensable to the modern parent who refused to accept the role of stay-at-home drudge!

Alas, once a little green consciousness creeps in, it's impossible to see them in the same light ever again. After the Women's Environmental Network launched their stunningly successful campaign against bleached paper products with *The Sanitary Protection Scandal* (the chlorine bleaching of paper in such products as disposable nappies, tea bags, sanitary towels and incontinence pads was causing the release of poisonous chemicals, including dioxin, into the environment), all disposable nappy

manufacturers switched to unbleached pulp, and pro-
claimed theirs to be the environment-friendly disposable.

This was a help, but two highly unpalatable facts
remain. These nappies are not disposable at all (in fact
they stay around, hoarding their contents for many years),
and they use up vast amounts of trees and plastic: one
fully-grown tree makes only 500 'disposables'. If a baby
needs roughly fifty nappies a week, that means a tree for
every ten weeks of nappied life – or five trees a year per
bottom.

In Britain, two-thirds of parents use 'disposables' and
three and a half billion are bought annually.

> 'Paper and plastic disposables have been cal-
> led an ecological disaster because of the vast
> quantities of woodpulp and plastic they
> require and the many problems associated
> with disposal. The green parent will choose a
> reusable alternative – better for your baby's
> future as well as for their bottom!'
> Women's Environmental Network in
> *Green Living*.

According to Karen Christensen, whose excellent book
Home Ecology gives a detailed run down of exactly what
you need to do to get back into cloth nappies, random
checks in a small American town found that a third of the
community's solid waste consisted of 'disposable'
nappies.

The health hazards from disposables are potentially far
greater than nappy rash. Nappies may be a source of
water contamination from landfill sites; Kristensen quotes

an American report which says that water containing viruses from human faeces – including live vaccines from routine childhood immunisations – can leach into the earth and pollute underground water supplies. In addition, airborne viruses may be carried by flies and other insects, contributing to an unhealthy and unsanitary situation.

ALTERNATIVELY . . .

If you do turn your back on disposables, you don't have to go back to the old cloth nappy system altogether: there are some interesting new alternatives. Women's Environmental Network recommend the felted wool Biobottoms as a better option than the traditional terry nappies and pins. These are machine washable nappy covers which hold a cloth nappy. They have velcro fastening strips and will last through about four or five nappy changes before they need to be washed. You will find Biobottoms in *The Whole Thing* catalogue; telephone 061 236 5116 to order a copy.

You could try a Danish alternative in the form of 'Wunderpants'. These are outer pants, made from specially treated wool which replace the old-fashioned plastic pants. Use them with traditional terries or muslin squares. The wool has a high lanoline content, so that any urine which comes into contact with it reacts with the lanolin. This produces a soap-like substance which neutralises the ammonia from the urine which causes nappy rash. At the same time this 'saponification' process keeps the pants hygienic. As long as the Wunderpants aren't soiled, they don't need to be washed: just air them for about twelve hours and they are ready for use again. When they do need a wash, it's handwashing with soap flakes at a low temperature. Wunderpants are available from Firstborn, 28 Claremont Avenue, Bristol, BS7 8JE (tel: 0272 240808).

The initial investment in cloth nappies and covers does seem like a big one – about £50 for proper daytime and night-time supplies of Wunderpants – but they are cheaper in the long run. Karen Christensen estimates that the expense of disposables adds up to about £1000 for a child potty trained by the age of two and a half. She works out that – even taking laundering into account – the cloth option costs half the disposable alternative. And apart from the odd replacement, future babies don't add to the expense.

Of course the cloth nappy system has its snags. When you take your baby out you need to carry a plastic bag within your nappy bag so that you can take soiled nappies home again. That makes travelling difficult, and child-minders may well be reluctant to take on anything but disposables. Yet, given the change of climate on the environmental front, disposables may soon become a source of quiet tut-tutting – a kind of bottom equivalent to the much-disapproved of child's dummy.

FINE TOOTH COMB

Parents with children at school will be familiar with the standard letter which their children bring home from time to time. 'Dear Parents, Beware head lice. Please use special louse killer lotion/shampoo brand X.' (In theory, parents can be prosecuted if they fail to get rid of head lice.)

But beware, parents, for brand X could be a far more serious hazard than 'nits'. Three pesticides are approved for use in the commonly-recommended shampoos: one is lindane, already banned from sheep dip. Because of new concerns that lindane may cause cancer it is being investigated by the government's advisory committee on pesticides. The other two are called carbaryl and malathion, which work chemically in ways similar to the nerve gases used in the First World War.

The Medical Entomology Centre at Cambridge University does not think the pesticides are a danger. Others are not sure, given that some people are very sensitive to pesticides.

The alternative treatment for head lice? The good old-fashioned fine tooth comb.

' "If I had to use any of the chemicals I would choose malathion first, and carbaryl second, but definitely not lindane," said Dr Hay [a lecturer in chemical pathology who has made a special study of pesticide poisoning]. "But surely, going through a child's hair with a comb is much better and grooming adds to a family's closeness." '

From the *Guardian*, October 1989.

GERM WARFARE

In many respects, because of the way they are built and because of the way we live in them, our homes can be very unsafe places for children. Some modern houses and blocks of flats have been built on top of old waste dumps, and dangerous fumes from the waste can seep into buildings for years afterwards. In recent decades, homes have been constructed with an alarming range of polluting and toxic chemicals, and we are persuaded to keep them 'clean' with a vast array of cleaning fluids, sprays and bleaches which are dangerous to children and to the environment.

You've seen the advertisement – or at least one very like it: kitchen floor is being mopped with New Improved Extra Super Powerful household cleaner; gorgeous blonde baby crawls across said kitchen floor, and previously guilty mum sighs with relief knowing that evil, life-threatening germs are not going to exterminate her little one.

But does the manufacturer tell parents that the arsenal of chemicals used in that cleaner may be more dangerous to baby than the dreaded germs? Not on your life. Yet floor cleaners often contain powerful chemicals such as ethanol, ammonia, formaldehyde and chlorine. These can kill if they are swallowed, so they aren't doing much good to babies and toddlers at floor level who put everything, from fingers to toys, into their mouths.

Parents, especially mothers, are under enormous pressure from advertisers to keep their homes 'germ free' – as if this were possible, or even desirable. If it's not the kitchen floor, it's the toilet, with its unfathomable potential for exploiting our most deep-seated fears of all things nasty, dark, dirty and lurking around the U-bend.

For years we have been encouraged to chuck bleach down our toilets, to squirt it into the crevices and wipe it around the seats. But bleach is one of the most polluting of all household chemicals. Yes, it does kill bacteria in the toilet. But it carries on killing them as it gets flushed into the sewage system, so that the benevolent bacteria, which digest our sewage and render it harmless, can't function. Large amounts of bleach can harm septic tank systems, and 'toilet fresheners' further pollute our water system.

'Many babies grow up surrounded by dangerous fumes from household disinfectants, used out of misplaced concern about hygiene. Most disinfectants contain cresol, a chemical which can affect the central nervous system and cause organ damage.'

Karen Christensen in *Home Ecology* (Arlington Books).

Bleach is also a very dangerous chemical in the home. For a start, there are the immediate risks of burning and poisoning to young children who may get hold of the bottle and dip their fingers in or take a swig . . . And if bleaches are ever mixed with other cleaners, lethal chlorine gas can form within a matter of seconds.

We also 'clean' our clothes and dishes, counter tops and

'Detergents are a very recent invention on this planet, and are at present being grossly abused. Nearly all of them contain phosphates. They all go down the drain and not only is this a terrible waste of phosphates, but it causes great damage to water life. The rivers and lakes of industrial countries, and the plants and creatures that live in them, are being destroyed by this excessive phosphate build up.'

John Seymour and Herbert Girardet in *Blueprint for a Green Planet* (Dorling Kindersley).

fridges, ovens, windows and furniture at a fast and furious rate. Yet chemical cleaners are harmful to the environment and to people. Most are oil based and made with toxic chemicals like hydrochloric acid, sulphuric acid and benzene. Many of them are tested on animals causing great distress, and are then heavily overpackaged.

BIN THE SPRAYS

Household 'cleaners' such as furniture polish, window cleaners and air fresheners do not have to be in aerosol form. We know now that the CFC gases (chlorofluorocarbons) used in such sprays break down the fragile ozone layer when they reach the upper atmosphere.

'There is simply no justification for using aerosols: they should be banned completely and immediately, but in default of such banning each one of us should simply make the decision not to use another one under any circumstances.'
John Seymour and Herbert Girardet in
Blueprint for a Green Planet
(Dorling Kindersley).

The ozone layer absorbs up to 99 per cent of the sun's ultraviolet rays so that we are protected from lethal levels of radiation on the ground. But the ozone layer is now thinning at an alarming rate. Signs of damage have already been spotted in plants and marine life, and every time the ozone layer decreases by one per cent, cases of skin cancer in people could rise by up to 3 per cent.

It is suspected also that the propellant gases in aerosol sprays cause cancer. The cans themselves cannot be recycled and they stand as a symbol of utter waste. So turn your back on the spray can: there are plenty of alternatives.

HANDS THAT DO DISHES . . .

As with other chemicals, ordinary detergents can be dangerous. Obviously, if you swallowed detergent directly it would make you pretty ill, causing nausea, vomiting and diarrhoea. But according to John Seymour and Herbert Girardet in *Blueprint for a Green Planet*, the drying agent which is designed to remain on the surface of crockery may increase the body's absorption of DDT and other pesticides present in food.

> 'Commercial air fresheners are particularly hazardous; they act by blocking our sense of smell with nerve deadening agents, and contain ingredients which are suspected carcinogens.'
> The Women's Environmental Network in
> *Green Living*.

Time was when most cleaning was done with soap and hot water. But soap – for hundreds of years made with natural ingredients – is now often full of added ingredients and perfumes. One of these is the bactericide hexachlorophane. In 1972, when a baby powder containing this chemical was used in a Paris hospital, thirty-six babies died and 150 children suffered long-term ill effects.

Investigations revealed that the product contained ten times the recommended amount of hexachlorophane – a manufacturer's error – and that it could be extremely dangerous even in small quantities.

Beware of the 'air fresheners' and synthetic perfumes which are supposed to improve our home environment, too. Their artificial perfumes consist simply of chemicals released into the air – a form of contamination. As for insecticides which kill insects by giving off vapours into your home, remember that anything which is poison to an insect is not likely to improve your children's health.

GREEN CLEAN

It's time to stop buying all these New Improved Super Strong chemical cleaners with their potential to poison our children and our world – and turn to some gentler, more natural alternatives.

- Refuse to be persuaded by the advertisers that we and our children and our houses are all so horribly dirty and smelly that only their products will make us socially acceptable. Is it really necessary to wash, clean and polish – yet? Can't it wait? For the parent whose natural tendency is to spend time with the children rather than on housework, there are now a host of environmental reasons to back you up!

- Try the Ecover alternative to chemical toilet cleaners and be soothed by the scents of lemon rather than dangerous fumes of bleach. Or, simply use a strong solution of vinegar which will break down limescale without causing pollution.

- Chlorine bleaches for clothes are not necessary either. Karen Christensen, the author of *Home Ecology*, recommends borax as an alternative: it can be bought from the chemist. She says that an American hospital tested a borax solution as a disinfectant and found that it satisfied their germicidal requirements. Borax can be used to whiten clothes and soften water. But beware: it is a poison. Alternatively, try the Ecover bleach.

- The old-fashioned washing-up liquids are full of phosphates which damage water life. (Phosphates are a rich food for minute water plants called algae. When phosphate levels are high, algae multiply fast, turning water into a thick green sludge which suffocates fish and other water life.) The new green alternatives are now widely on sale, with gentler, natural ingredients.

  Otherwise, you could try simple soap and hot water. Some green housekeepers are keen on the 'soap jar', in which you collect all the left-over scraps of soap. If you pour boiling water onto your soap scraps you get a soft soapy jelly which can be used for washing up or handwashing. Or try this soda and soap recipe. It can also be used for washing clothes – and as a homemade shampoo:

  > Cut up a cake of pure soap and bring it to boil in a little water. Then mash it up. Dissolve one cup of washing soda in a little hot water and put it in a bucket. Add the soap solution, divide into three buckets and fill up with water. It will set into a soft gel. Use two cups per wash.

- Standard washing powders also pollute water with phosphates and may irritate the skin. Phosphate-free alternatives are now available even in the big supermarkets. The 'green' washing powders (like Ecover) do cost more – but you use far less. Or return to a bit of simple handwashing with soap now and then. And think twice before chucking clothes into the laundry basket: the advent of washing machines has made it all too easy to wash clothes when it's not really necessary. Try airing them overnight and go over them with a clothes brush. Babies' clothes especially may only need a quick rinse rather than the whole complicated, energy-burning cycle.

• That spray-on plastic shine for furniture, with its accompanying synthetic smell, are no longer a must for every houseproud houseperson. Indeed, the aerosol polishes containing silicone are accused of giving instant shine without filling scratches, until they build up to a milky coating that has to be removed by stripping the furniture. Instead try a mixture of one part lemon juice with two parts olive oil. It looks like salad dressing, but if you rub it into your furniture with a soft cloth you'll get a glowing and fragrant result. Or try the National Trust's Furniture Wax from NT shops, which you only need to use once or twice a year.

• Glass and tiles can be polished with a fifty-fifty mixture of white vinegar and water. Squirt it from a spray bottle and wipe with a cloth. Mixed with salt or baking soda, this vinegar will also polish brass and copper.

• If you're a stickler for keeping the silver candelabra burnished to a high shine, eschew the commercial metal cleaners with their ammonia and hazardous fumes. Polish silver with bicarbonate of soda and a soft cloth. Try lemon juice on brass and copper, and cider vinegar on chrome.

• Air freshener? The best variety is fresh air. Failing that – especially in colder weather when you've got your home well insulated – try a pot-pourri made of dried flower petals, spices and natural oils. Poppy Pathway Aromatics (tel: 0234 848622) makes ceramic rings to fit over bulbs on table lamps: you put a few drops of aromatic oil on the ring and when the light is turned on fragrance permeates the room.

That most durable of all pot plants the spider plant also has a tonic effect on the air, with its ability to absorb indoor toxins. They are also easy and fun for children to plant and water. All plants and vases of flowers give off water and oxygen and so improve the quality of air in your home. For a more high-tech alternative, invest in an ioniser. These machines can help sufferers from hayfever, migraine and bronchitis.

- Remember that two common household products with wide cleaning potential are bicarbonate of soda and plain old table salt. Bicarb (which can be bought in large bags from the chemist) can be used as a bathroom scouring powder, a water softener, a toothpowder and chrome polisher. Salt can also be used as a slightly disinfectant, abrasive scouring powder. Try keeping your drains clear by pouring a handful of salt or bicarb down the sink with a kettle of boiling water.
- Instead of the chemical insecticides, with their dangerous toxins, try hanging bunches of herbs – like bay leaves, mint or pennyroyal. Citrus oil is also an insect repellant. And don't forget the old-fashioned fly swatter.
- For cleaning floors of cork, tile, lino or slate, add half a cup of vinegar to a bucket of water. Or try the fragrant Ecover alternative floor cleaner.
- Clean your fridge and around the cooker hotplates with bicarb and a damp cloth. Ditto for china, plastic and crockery.

PET PROBLEMS

Much as children love to play with household pets, cats and dogs and other furry varieties can increase food

poisoning risks. They can also cause the diseases toxocariasis and toxoplasmosis, which can cause serious
problems such as blindness in children.

When the dog licks your toddler's hand, just think what
it might have been licking a little earlier. Or what the cat is
also sitting on when it sits on the kitchen counter . . .
Sometimes pets eat out of rubbish bins which can be a
source of food poisoning bacteria.

> 'If toxoplasmosis is contracted by a pregnant
> woman, it can cause congenital problems
> such as blindness, deafness and brain damage
> in the baby. It is twenty times more common
> than rubella, but no routine antenatal blood
> test is offered in this country.'
> Megan Harrison in *New Generation*, the
> journal of the National Childbirth Trust,
> September 1989.

Cats can spread toxoplasmosis through their faeces,
while dogs and cats can spread toxocariasis. Make sure
pets are wormed every three months and make sure
everyone in the family washes their hands before eating.
The National Childbirth Trust's journal *New Generation*
recommends that pregnant women should not empty cat
litter trays in case they inadvertently touch faeces. Also
keep litter trays out of the way of toddlers and babies who
will treat them as a kind of sandpit to play in.

As a general rule, keep pets away from food and
kitchen work surfaces. Put their beds somewhere other
than the kitchen, and don't give them food or drink in
bowls that will later be used by the family. You can get

further information from the Toxoplasmosis Trust, 46 Ashburnham Place, London SE10 8UG (tel: 081 692 2599); also, Community Hygiene Concern, Worm Watch Toxocara Information Pack, 32 Crane Avenue, Isleworth, Middlesex TW7 7JL.

SAFE AS HOUSES

Time was when homes were built from natural materials culled from the local environment – bricks, stone, wood and thatch. Their furnishings were made from natural materials too, like wood, cotton and wool. Life may not have been as comfortable as it is today, but at least people could rest assured that the materials of their home were not going to damage their health.

The same is not true today when more and more of the newly-invented synthetic substances used in houses are coming under suspicion. Recently, the expression 'sick building syndrome' has come into the language as scientists begin to investigate building materials which are thought to bring a host of maladies upon the people who work or live within them.

According to Brian Price, co-author of the guide to household chemical hazards *C for Chemicals*, we tend to assume that if a chemical is on sale it is safe. Yet only a fraction of the 60,000-odd chemicals we commonly use in our homes have been tested for safety. And these tests are usually based on the tolerance levels of healthy young men.

Women who are pregnant, women who are trying to conceive, and young children may be especially vulnerable. Young children breathe in proportionately more air than adults and their lungs are better at extracting pollutants such as toxic gases, leaded dust and solvent vapours. Yet hydrocarbons and other solvents have been linked with birth defects – and these can occur when either the mother or the father has been exposed to the hazard. Such chemicals are found in adhesives, paints, wood treatments and many DIY and household products.

'Houses have been transformed by synthetic materials. A large proportion of the plastics produced by the chemical industry end up in the home, as tabletops, foam mattresses, cushions, furniture, fabrics, wallpaper and so on, while in decorating we use many chemicals that were unknown a few decades ago. Quite what side-effects all these will have, no one really knows.'

John Seymour and Herbert Girardet in
Blueprint for a Green Planet
(Dorling Kindersley).

We now know that asbestos – once hailed as the perfect building material – is highly dangerous and that asbestos fibres can cause lung cancer. But there are many other new products coming onto the market every year which carry risks we can only guess at.

Plastics, which are used more and more in modern homes, not only cause pollution to the atmosphere in their production process, but some of them – like PVC – pollute the atmosphere of your home once they are in place. Fumes from solvents, paints and other household chemicals add to the fug. These days more people are killed by the toxic fumes given off by house fires than by the effects of fire itself.

'In 1982, a founder member of the US Formaldehyde Victim's Association spoke to a special commission of the House of Representatives about its effects. She explained how her whole family had suffered from chronic colds, tiredness and throat inflammation. Her husband was affected by a crippling bout of arthritis. Her children were unable to concentrate and to take on what they were taught at school. All this was a result of using chipboard panels containing formaldehyde for dividing walls.'

John Seymour and Herbert Girardet in
Blueprint for a Green Planet
(Dorling Kindersley).

Perhaps the most notorious of air-poisoners in the modern home – apart from cigarette smoke – is formaldehyde. This material is found in insulating foams, synthetic varnishes, disinfectants, medicines, plywood glues, chipboard and hardboard, washing detergent, wallpaper, fabric and carpet finishes and even some cosmetics. Formaldehyde is released very slowly, seeping out of materials in the home. It is a potent irritant, affecting the eyes, nose, throat and lungs; it can cause headaches, depression and dizziness, sometimes triggering extreme chemical sensitivity. According to the Women's Environmental Network, around one in five people is sensitive to the toxic effects of formaldehyde, and the rest of us are likely to be affected to some degree. Even in very small concentrations, it can cause defects of the nervous system and memory loss. It has now been banned from some products in Canada, the USA and West Germany, but most countries still allow its unrestrained use. Urea-formaldehyde insulating foam – banned in the USA and elsewhere – is still common in Britain.

LICK OF PAINT

Paint is also a very polluting substance – together with paint solvents. Modern paints are not as toxic as the old-fashioned varieties but chemicals slowly released by modern paints can cause a number of health problems. Painting a radiator in a small room – says Brian Price in *C for Chemicals* – can lead to very high concentrations of noxious fumes as the paint cures.

And the paint industry is responsible for widespread water pollution. Lead is now restricted in paint, but now other dangerous substances, like cadmium and titanium dioxide, have taken its place. Titanium dioxide is the pigment used in making white paints, and its toxic by-products include various heavy metals as well as sulphuric acid and chlorinated hydrocarbons to such an extent that the toxic wastes of the paint industry have become a major environmental problem in recent decades.

Paint removers, strippers and other solvents generally contain poisonous hydrocarbons – members of the same chemical group that contains many pesticides. These are dangerous to health if inhaled, and if substances like white spirit and paint stripper are poured down the drain they end up at the sewage treatment works, where they poison the 'good' bacteria which decompose the sewage waste.

Wood treatments are another minefield of chemical danger. For many years lindane and dieldrin have been used as woodworm killers, but both are highly toxic and lindane has been linked with leukaemia. They are both highly poisonous to bats and their use in attics has been blamed for the sad decline in the bat population. As bats are a protected species, it is illegal to use lindane in a roof where bats are known to roost. The authors of *C for Chemicals* recommend avoiding all lindane-based products.

First you need to ask yourself, do we really need to paint it? In the teeth of the extraordinary modern mania for DIY, it is worth reminding yourself that all moral virtues do not necessarily reside in a coat of fresh paint. Indeed, environmental virtues may well reside in doing nothing, given the enormous pollution caused by the paint industry.

True, the nest-building prerogative is strong, but it seems strange that so many parents want to show they care by bringing their children into the world while up to their arms in poisonous paints and solvents. And there are alternatives to the standard commercial paints. Organic, lead-free and non-toxic paints are available from Auro, Saffron Walden, Essex (tel: 0799 24744) who also supply oils and furniture waxes.

All household paints made since 1986 are lead-free. But old paints may have a high lead content. It is well known that lead can damage the brains of small children, so make sure that you don't sand down old paint while they are around. Paint strippers will get round the problem of lead particles in the air after sanding down old paint, but of course the strippers themselves give off toxic vapour. Make sure that children are not at hand and that the room is well ventilated.

Take care when throwing away paint, paint scrapings and solvents. Your local authority may operate a special facility for disposing of household chemical waste: if they don't, wrap them up and put them in the dustbin. But as a general rule, the less you use of these substances, the better.

IDEAL HOMES

With the explosion of environmental concern at the end of the 1980s, various groups have turned their attention to home life and what all of us can do to cut down on pollution.

Friends of the Earth and SustainAbility (the green growth company which promotes environmentally sustainable economic growth) came up with their own Green Kitchen for the *Daily Mail* Ideal Home Exhibition. *Good Housekeeping* magazine came up with a 'Green Kitchen' supplement. And the Women's Environmental Network toured the country with their Green Home Exhibition.

> 'The Green Kitchen does not contain a microwave oven. Although they cook food more quickly than conventional equipment, microwaves are primarily suited to pre-prepared, processed foods. Home prepared, organic meals are better for the environment and are more nutritious and tastier too!'
> Women's Environmental Network in
> *Green Living*.

For anyone who once thought that being green was a load of old lentils, the WEN exhibition finally put paid to that idea. Here is a very classy, very stylish set of rooms that any yuppie could well be proud of: classic, comfortable furniture, upholstered in unbleached cottons, finished with natural oils and waxes; a warm tile and wood furnished kitchen, stocked with the latest in energy-saving appliances; a bright smart bathroom sporting an array of non-toxic cleaning products, cruelty-free cosmetics and herbal and homeopathic remedies.

The WEN exhibition draws attention to the range of 'white goods' that are now using the most up-to-date technology to stay on the right side of the green consumer. They chose the Zanussi gas cooker, which uses one-third of the energy of electric cookers.

As for cookware, the old-fashioned, energy-saving pressure cooker gets the thumbs up – as long as it is stainless steel and not aluminium. WEN says that aluminium cooking pans and teapots should be avoided because recent research links aluminium in our diets to senile dementia. Although they cost more, stainless steel, cast iron and enamelled cookware is safer and will last much longer.

The WEN Green Home also has a Zanussi fridge-freezer and washing machine. Both of these are highly energy efficient. The fridge has half the CFCs of other fridges in the insulating foam (see Pollution), while the washing machine has been especially adapted to use less detergent. It is also capable of saving water, by selecting the right amount to suit the weight of the clothes in the wash.

For full details of the WEN Green Home, contact Women's Environmental Network, 287 City Road, London EC1 VLA (tel: 071 490 2511), or send for their *Green Living* publication, which is all about the exhibition.

THE BIOLOGICAL HOME

As we become more and more aware of the dangers of synthetic building and furnishing materials in our homes,

Good wood

Half the world's animal and plant species are found in the tropical rainforests which are also home to thousands of people. At least 100 acres of rain forest are now being cleared each minute with disastrous economic and social consequences. Native people are being forcibly resettled and some fifty species of wildlife are becoming extinct every day. If the destruction isn't stopped, all the forests could disappear within fifteen years.

Apart from clearing land to graze cattle, the rainforests are being destroyed to get hold of their valuable timber. So if you don't want to be part of the problem, don't buy tropical hardwoods, like teak, mahogany, ramin and iroko. There are plenty of alternatives, like the faster growing softwoods, pine, larch and spruce. Check the Friends of the Earth *Good Wood Guide* before you go shopping, obtainable from FoE.

natural and organic alternatives are coming to the fore. In Germany, Austria and Scandinavia, a new type of 'biological' architecture is gaining ground. The idea is to choose natural materials wherever possible: bricks rather than concrete; natural insulators, like glass fibre, paper or cork, rather than plastic foams; natural floor coverings, like wool and traditional linoleum, rather than synthetics.

In the 'natural' home, doors and cupboards are made from wood (which is sustainably harvested) rather than wood chips or fibres held together with glues – which will give off fumes for years to come. Furniture is joined in the traditional manner rather than glued together. Paint – when it is used – is made from natural ingredients such as lime. Wood surfaces are treated with wax rather than synthetic varnishes.

Of course we don't all have the luxury of building our own natural dream home from scratch, but there are many aspects of biological architecture that we can incorporate into our DIY habits and daily lives.

And the commercial potential of the householders' lean towards green is now being picked up by industry. In September 1989, *Marketing* magazine ran a series on green consumption, detailing the kind of products that the shoppers of the 1990s will want in their homes. *Marketing* expect a 'revolution for marketers, even for a nation of pale green homes'. They predict changes on every level – such as the demise of paper tissues and the return of the cloth hanky. Biros must be refillable, vacuum cleaners must be fitted with microfilters to remove pollutants, ovens (preferably gas) must contain super-efficient insulation, and the quality and durability of all products will be an acceptable and vital weapon against waste.

2

Food

*food fears * practical protection*
*chemical dangers * organic food*
*Parents for Safe Food * baby food*
*milk and juice * processed foods*
*meat * irradiation * tea and coffee*
*shops * free food *

GROANS FROM THE TABLE

There are times when there seems to be nothing we can give our children to eat that isn't somehow risky. That brown bread we encouraged them to eat could be tainted with pesticides, their boiled eggs with salmonella, those yoghurts with botulism, those baked potatoes with tecnazene, and those apples – symbol of health and purity – might give them cancer.

And there are few subjects that parents are more sensitive about than their children's food. From the moment a baby is born, food takes on mammoth significance, both practical and symbolic. At first, it's a question of whether to breastfeed or bottlefeed: until recently the breastfeeders were winning in the 'Good Mother' stakes. But now the newspapers tell us that breastmilk contains so much of the deadly chemical dioxin that it would never be put on sale in the shops.

'Independent toxicologists have been saying for years now, that salmonella will become a rampant epidemic; the disease is inevitable, when intensively-reared chickens are kept in Auschwitz-type conditions, and fed on their own faeces, and the ground up remains of other chickens. Those of us who care about the welfare of animals see the soaring rate of salmonella poisoning as the mild revenge of a tortured chicken population.'

From *Living Earth*, Spring 1989.

As babies grow into childhood, the spectres of sugar, salt, saturated fat, additives, colourings, hormones, antibiotics and processes emerge *ad nauseam*: 'Why can't I have biscuits/cakes/sweets/sausages/burgers/fizzy drinks, Mum? All my friends do.' And so it goes on as mothers (mostly) try not to be seen to strain every nerve to get their children to eat even a mouthful of green vegetables. Until they read that their cabbage has been sprayed with carbendazim, captan and lindane (capable of causing either/or cancer, birth defects, genetic mutations . . .).

For food is inextricably linked with children's well-being as well as our sense of ourselves as capable, nurturing parents. Which is why so many parents have reacted with such horror and anger to the wave of news stories about what is being done to food for the purposes of profit. We try so hard to feed our children healthily – only to find that our 'good' food was contaminated at source. It is appalling and quite unacceptable that we can't give our children even the basics in fruit and vegetables without the worry that in the long term we might also be giving them cancer.

And not only is modern food production capable of poisoning our children but its very manufacture is poisoning our children's environment.

FOOD ACTION

The good news is that people are demanding change, and the more we discover what is being done to our food the more we vote with our purses – against unsafe and unhealthy food. As one food scandal followed another through the 1980s, consumers have begun to buy healthier food, shops have scrambled to prove how healthy their produce is, and a series of media and consumer campaigns have mercilessly hounded the culprits.

When the television personality and comedienne Pamela Stephenson appeared on the box objecting to the use of the cancer-causing chemical 'alar' on apples, the pressure group Parents for Safe Food was born. Twenty thousand concerned parents wrote to express their concern, and the campaign culminated in the withdrawal of alar by its manufacturers.

Since 1985 the London Food Commission has set up a vigorous and effective public information campaign. It is still Britain's only independent food and public health watchdog, and they have had their hands full from the word go with BST (the milk hormone), BSE ('mad cow' disease), food irradiation, cook-chill, additives, pesticide residues, poverty, the needs of Black and ethnic minorities – to name but some areas of their work. The London Food Commission can be contacted at 88 Old Street,

London EC1V 9AR (tel: 071 253 9513). They provide an excellent range of books and leaflets.

As soon as consumers have been given accurate information – and the level of official secrecy in Britain is notorious – they have responded. A Friends of the Earth survey found in 1985 that people were keen to buy organic food and prepared to pay more for it. Since then more and more people have been quietly demonstrating that, for the sake of their children and the sake of their planet, they want healthier food.

TEN STEPS PAST THE PITFALLS OF FOOD ...

- **Don't panic!** Your children's daily nourishment won't kill them tomorrow. Children are amazingly resilient and can survive on a diet of virtually anything for long periods. On the other hand, if you can encourage them to eat healthier food, it is the sooner the better for their long-term health.
- **Taste** food before giving it to young children. Aside from the recent scares about metal and glass fragments in processed food, it's worth sampling all their food to see if it tastes good. Much of the baby food sold in tins, bottles or packets as 'hearty lamb stew' or 'chicken with spring vegetables' tastes more like wallpaper paste. If you don't like it, why should they? Bin it before your baby chucks it at the wall – and start again with the variety and flavours of real food. With the exception of eggs and salt, there is no reason why babies shouldn't eat much the same food (fruit, vegetables, lean meat and fish) that you do – after mashing or liquidizing.
- **Wash** all fruit and vegetables before eating or cooking. Not all pesticide residues can be removed this way,

but it's a minimum precaution. Peeling skins will also help avoid some pesticide residues, but the snag is you may also lose some valuable nutrients.

- **Buy organic food** and wholefoods wherever you can find them, and whenever you can afford them. This is really the only way to avoid most of the risks from pesticides, additives and so on. It supports the organic growers too, and lets the big food manufacturers know that we've had enough of their technofood.

- **Prepare your own food:** take those old cookbooks off the shelf and dust them down. It does take longer but at least you know what has happened to the food before it reaches the family table. The shorter the journey from soil to dinner plates, the fresher and more nourishing it will be – and think of the energy saved in avoiding all that packaging, processing, refrigeration, transport and reheating.

- **Balance and moderation in all things.** There has to be a sort of 'safety in numbers' with food: if you don't give the family too much of anything, there's less risk that they will get too many of the nasty elements in any one food. You will also be giving them a wider range of nutrients and getting them used to different food.

- **Local produce:** whenever you have a choice, buy the simpler, less processed variety of food – and the one that is produced nearby. It will be better for your family's health and better for the world beyond your kitchen.

- **Read the labels** on cans and packets: the longer the list, the more heavily processed they will be. The current labelling laws mean that the contents of everything we buy must be listed in order of size, but we don't have to be told the exact percentage of each. Beware the word 'natural': it has no legal definition and can be misleading. 'No artificial additives' can mean that 'natural' additives – such as chemicals from insects and wood – have been put in. If a food such as jelly is labelled 'orange flavour', it may have no orange in it whatsoever. If it is called 'orange jelly' or 'orange flavoured', its flavour must come from oranges. Sugar can be disguised under other names – including glucose, fructose, lactose, invert syrup, dextrose and maltose.

- **Real meat:** ask your butcher or supermarket manager where the meat you buy has been produced – and if it has been produced humanely. Support farmers who use humane methods, like the Real Meat Company (see page 67), and try using less meat and more beans and pulses in your cooking.
- **Home grown:** avoid buying food which has been produced overseas when a home-grown alternative is available. You will be avoiding a waste of resources on transport, storage and distribution. Local food is likely to be fresher, too.

KAMIKAZE CHEMICALS

Some 150 pesticides currently in use in Britain leave residues on our food. Not every parent or child washes these off – and some of them can't be washed or peeled off as they have been incorporated into the food. A quarter of the pesticides used in Britain (many are banned overseas) are suspected of causing cancers. Others have been linked with genetic mutations, birth defects, allergies and even death.

Some scientists say there is little risk. The Ministry of Agriculture, which now admits there are pesticide residues in all our food, even in mothers' breastmilk, says the amounts are so small as to be insignificant.

Yet in the USA new evidence shows that children under five are especially at risk. The National Resources Defense Council, one of America's most respected environmental organizations, reported in May 1989 that some 5,500 American children would eventually develop cancer directly from apples sprayed with the chemical alar. The American authorities decided to ban alar, and the manufacturers, Uniroyal, withdrew the chemical from the American market. But despite demands from Parents For Safe Food, the British Ministry of Agriculture repeatedly said the spray was safe. Eventually, Uniroyal withdrew alar in Britain at the end of 1989, after tests had linked it to tumours in animals.

So just how harmful are crop sprays? As yet, we don't know. There have been no adequate long-term studies of what happens to a person's health after a lifetime's ingestion of low doses of pesticides. Nor do we know what effects these agrochemicals have in combination – although 'cocktails' of chemicals can have increased effects on animals.

We do know that many of these chemicals are highly poisonous. Some are related to nerve gases, strong poisons and depressants of the immune system. And most cases of illegal spraying – such as a farmer spraying his crops too near the date of harvest – are never detected.

Again, at the beginning of 1990, the American manufacturers of a range of fungicides (used for spraying on crops like apples, beans, cabbage, berries, lettuces, melons, oats and strawberries) told American farmers to stop using their sprays on these crops. The same fungicides have been widely used in Britain for nearly forty years on a similar range of crops, but British farmers have been given no comparable warning.

'Brown bread sampled in 1984–6 [by the Ministry of Agriculture] showed a 58 per cent contamination with residues, and in 1987 showed a 72 per cent contamination rate; bran in 1984–6 contained residues in 54 per cent of samples, and in 1987 in 93 per cent of samples, whilst wheatgerm products showed organophosphate residues in 54 per cent of samples. But you can't avoid pesticides by eating white bread. 67 per cent of white bread samples contained residues.

'The most worrying finding was the high incidence of contamination of infant rusks with organophosphates, 58 per cent contained residues – some of two or three different pesticides . . . We just don't know what the long term effects may be, particularly in young children, of many years' intake of even trace residues of organophosphates.'

From an article by Dr David Hodges in the Soil Association's journal *Living Earth*, July/September 1989.

The action taken by manufacturers in the USA follows threats by the EPA (Environmental Protection Agency) to ban the use of the 'EBDC' (Ethylene Bisdithiocarbonate) family of fungicides. According to a report in the *Guardian* in November 1989, by James Erlichman, the agency believes that continued use of the EBDCs may cause at least 125,000 extra cancer cases in the USA. Children are thought to be most at risk because they eat a lot of fruit, are small and have plenty of time to develop cancer.

According to Erlichman, scientists are most concerned about ETU (ethylene thiourea), a breakdown chemical found in the fungicides which causes cancer in animals and accumulates most in heat-treated foods like tomato paste, ketchup and apple juice.

The Soil Association – which promotes organic, chemical-free farming – won't use the phrase 'pesticide-free food'. It believes it's no longer possible to grow entirely pesticide-free food in this country, because the levels of background contamination in the soil, water and atmosphere are now too high.

Britain is obliged under European law to set Maximum Residue Limits (MRLs) for pesticide residues on fruit and vegetables. But MRLs have not been set for all pesticides. Tecnazene, the potato pesticide, has no MRL despite its current, lavish use. The government claims there is no health risk from tecanzene, but campaigners argue that it may be linked to cancers and birth defects. It is also harmful to fish.

GOING ORGANIC

Organic food is safer, healthier and often tastier – but still more expensive – than the standard produce which graces our supermarket shelves. It is grown without the arsenal of chemicals used in most of our food production, and offers the closest thing to pesticide-free food that we can give to our children.

The Soil Association was founded as a charity in 1946 to further a philosophy of 'interrelated wholeness', encouraging an ecological approach to agriculture. It promotes organic growing as the only long-term option to the chemical farming which is causing havoc to the environment. It also operates the 'Symbol Scheme' which licenses commercial food production to organic standards and acts as a consumer guarantee of organic quality.

'Our health depends on the quality of our food – the plant and animal products we eat. The quality of our food depends on the health of the soil. This vital relationship is crucial to the future of life on this planet.'

The Soil Association

WHERE TO BUY ORGANIC FOOD

First try your local wholefood shop, market or farm shop for locally-grown organic produce. Failing that, most of the big supermarkets now have an organic section. If yours doesn't yet, why not ask for one?

'Buy organically-grown foods. Nitrate pollution from artificial fertilizers now threatens one third of this country's water supplies, leading to potential cancer hazards and particular dangers to babies and unborn children. The use of fertilizers is increasing, so the problem will get much worse in the next few years as the residues enter the water table.'

From *The Green Alternative*, edited by Peter Bunyard and Fern Morgan-Grenville (Methuen).

There are various lists and directories of organic suppliers. Try *The New Organic Food Guide* which lists over 600 organic shops, wholesalers and farms in Great Britain. It's written by Alan Gear (of the television show 'All Muck and Magic') who is head of the Henry Doubleday Research Association at Ryton. Write to the association at the National Centre for Organic Gardening, Ryton-On-Dunsmore, Coventry CV8 3LG (tel: 0203 303517).

The Soil Association also has a list of organic farmers and growers in your area or nationally (price £2 and £10 respectively). They publish a 'Safe Meat' list too for £2. They can be found at 86–8 Colston Street, Bristol, Avon BS1 5BB (tel: 0272 290661).

ORGANIC SYMBOLISM

Food that is grown to organic standards qualifies for both the Soil Association Symbol and for the international 'Farm Verified Organic' label which ensures that food grown outside this country is organic. (Alas, two-thirds of organic food sold in Britain is produced abroad where governments are often far more supportive of organic growers.) If you buy organic food in bulk it may also be labelled 'Organic Growers Association' and/or 'Organic Farmers and Growers', which are both highly reputable organizations.

ORGANIC CAMPAIGNING

In 1989, the Soil Association launched a campaign aimed at the turn of the century: they want to see 20 per cent of British farming organic by the year 2000. They claim it is possible to revolutionize British agriculture using available farming techniques and without straining the government's budget. The Soil Association also believes that consumer demand for organic food could reach the 20 per cent mark by the year 2000.

Guidelines

The guidelines for organic growing were set out in 1981 by the International Federation of Organic Agriculture Movements:

- To work as much as possible within a closed system, and to draw upon local resources.
- To maintain the long-term fertility of soils.
- To avoid all forms of pollution that may result from agricultural techniques.
- To produce foodstuffs of the highest nutritional quality and sufficient quantity.
- To reduce the use of fossil energy in agricultural practice to a minimum.
- To give livestock conditions of life that conform to their physiological needs and to humanitarian principles.
- To make it possible for agricultural producers to earn a living through their work and develop their potentialities as human beings.

A switch to organic would help to cut overproduction. According to the Soil Association, in 1988 people in Britain paid an average of £137 per head just to get rid of surplus food they didn't need. Changing to organic grow-ing, they say, would – in the long run – be cheaper than this continuing support for too much food.

'Safe Meat' is also a campaigning issue for the Soil Association, and they list shops and farms where you can buy organic meat (see 'Real Meat' below).

PESTICIDES AND PARENTS FOR SAFE FOOD

Parents for Safe Food is recommending parents to buy organic fruit, juices and vegetables, to talk to supermarket managers about the issue and to wash – or even peel – all produce before eating it. They suggest training yourself to be content with less 'perfect' looking produce: this look is achieved with pesticides and is merely cosmetic. They also want parents to write to their MPs, MEPs and the Prime Minister, requesting support for pure food.

'The real message of hope in all this, is the organic message. We are now saying to our supermarkets and greengrocers "We don't want our products laden with pesticides. We demand to know exactly what is in our food and drink. We want you to label all food and drink with the pesticides that have been used on them. We want you to monitor pesticide residues and, particularly, we want you to supply us with certified organic produce. We want it to be more widely available – in greater quantity and at lower prices." '

Pamela Stephenson, of Parents for Safe Food, in *Living Earth*, September 1989.

The group is also calling on the government:

- to provide financial incentives to farmers to make the switch to organic agriculture
- for more independent research, testing, and monitoring of agrochemicals: how are they used, and what residues do they leave?
- for pesticide labelling
- for full access to information about pesticides
- for the choice of a safe alternative in the form of cheaper, more plentiful organic food
- for full representation on the committees which approve and regulate pesticides.

For more information, get in touch with Parents for Safe Food, Britannia House, 1–11 Glenthorne Road, London W6 0LF (tel: 081 748 9898).

BABY FOOD

Some of the nastier bits of news to come out of the late 1980s concerned baby foods which had been contaminated deliberately by blackmailers. But the reports also conveyed the odd impression that these commercially-produced jars and powders for infants are their only source of food.

According to the London Food Commission, the government's report on residues published in March 1989 showed that 25 per cent of baby foods tested contained pesticide residues. Two of these samples were infant formulas. In Britain, manufacturers are not obliged to test for these residues, and they don't have to say whether they have tested or not.

Why not avoid the risks of these foods by giving your baby the best of your own food, preferably organic, and

'In 1986, Heinz declared in America that it would be removing all pesticide residues from their baby products, listing twelve chemicals which were in current use on farms. All crops would be examined for pesticides before being accepted.

'Some of the same chemicals are used in farms in Europe, but Heinz has not announced a ban on their presence in baby food here. Milupa, on the other hand, claims that all its ingredients are examined for pesticides, and the meats are also examined for hormone levels.'

Tim Lobstein in *Children's Food*.
(Unwin Paperbacks).

avoiding salt, strong flavourings and eggs until they are a bit older. Try apples, carrots, bananas, avocados, potatoes, beans and peas: mashed or puréed, babies will lap them up.

BREAST IS STILL BEST

When even women's breastmilk is contaminated by modern pollutants, then surely there is no longer any room for complacency on environmental issues.

While breastfeeding is still the best way to care for babies, with its incalculable emotional and nutritional advantages, it is disturbing to realize that women now have dioxin in their breastmilk. Dioxin has been linked to cancers in humans and animals, and to mass fish deaths. Dioxins come from a variety of sources, such as industrial incineration and waste metal processing plants, effluent from pulp and paper mills, leaded petrol and paper goods – like food packaging and milk cartons.

There is no 'safe level' of dioxin in the human body – or in the environment – and dioxin is generally considered to be the most dangerous chemical known (it is 10,000 times more poisonous than cyanide). According to the Women's Environmental Network, levels of dioxin in women's breastmilk are 100 times greater than the stipulated British safety guidelines.

> 'Dioxin does not dilute in the environment but tends to concentrate in wildlife and sediments. It is then able to build up in the food chain. The levels found in mothers' breastmilk by studies sponsored by the World Health Organisation in 1988, show that dioxin has already reached the top of the food chain and children today are receiving much higher doses than those of their parents.'
>
> From *Dioxin*, *A Briefing*, Women's Environmental Network.

The Women's Environmental Network argues that government must take urgent action on dioxins, and manufacturers must be pressured to change the way they operate.

What can you do?

- Write to your MP to let him know how concerned you are about dioxins.
- Buy unbleached, chlorine-free paper products where they are available.

● Ask supermarkets and shops for unbleached food packaging.

For more information contact Women's Environmental Network, 287 City Road, Islington, London EC1V 1LA (tel: 071 490 2511).

Remember that formula milk is far from ideal for babies with its aluminium content, and the problem of contaminants in the water used to make it. Also, for every three million bottlefed babies, 70,000 tonnes of metal are used up in discarded milk tins. Breastmilk involves no wastage; it is cheap and naturally hygienic (try Gabrielle Palmer's *The Politics of Breastfeeding*, published by Pandora Press, for more information).

Canada's 26,000 Arctic dwellers, the Inuit (or 'Eskimos'), have become contaminated by Polychlorinated biphenyls passed through breast milk. Developed in 1929 to cool electrical transformers, 'PCBs' have been carried on the wind from industrial countries to the Arctic. PCBs can cause cancer and damage to the immune and reproductive systems and the brain.

GOTTA LOTTA BOTTLE

As they get older, children drink a great deal of milk (of the cow variety). We're already producing too much milk, yet the drug companies have come up with a new, genetically-engineered hormone called BST (bovine somatotrophin) which will enable farmers to get 7 to 14 per cent more out of their cows.

BST is already being used in secret tests on some British cows, and their milk is mixed in with all the rest. The producers claim that there are no health risks to humans. But BST's opponents – which include consumer groups, animal welfare organizations and farmers across Europe – don't agree. They say that BST could harm human health: cows injected with the hormone require more concentrates which will add more pesticide residues and fungal toxins to the milk. BST can also harm cows' health, causing increased mastitis (painful udder inflamation) and generally putting strain on the cow. The pressure to produce even more milk will make cows more vulnerable to disease, which means they will be given more drugs.

And milk quality may also be affected: only healthy animals produce healthy milk and BST milk may have a lower protein content and have reduced levels of other important nutritional elements (like orotic acid). BST also represents a further step towards high-tech farming with cows kept in intensive large-scale units on even more drugs.

Write to your MP or your milk supplier to let them know that you don't want BST in your milk. A consumer boycott of BST would make them think again. And, if BST is licensed, demand that milk from treated cows is labelled as such.

For further information contact Compassion in World Farming, 20 Lavant Street, Petersfield, Hampshire GU32 3EW (tel: 0730 64208) and the London Food Commission.

BANK ON BOTTLES

A New Zealand government study has found that milk sold in paper cartons contains dioxin, whereas milk in glass bottles showed no traces at all. This dangerous and cancer-inducing chemical is thought to travel from the bleached paper cartons through the polythene linings and into milk. It could even be that the polythene helps this 'leaching' to happen. New Zealand manufacturers are now changing to unbleached cartons. But their British counterparts don't seem willing to follow suit.

What can you do? Buy milk in glass bottles – which are also recyclable; write to your MP; and ask shops and supermarkets to make a stand for their customers.

LOOSELY JUICE

Many of the bottles and cartons of drink which children find so attractive are loosely described as 'fruit drinks', but in fact some of them contain little or no fruit juice. When the London Food Commission's *Food Magazine* tested a range of thirty-seven brands, they found that half contained less than 10 per cent fruit juice, and several so-called 'hi-juice' drinks had less than 20 per cent juice. So what do they contain? The answer is water, sugar, colouring, flavouring, stabilizers and artificial sweeteners – in varying proportions.

To make sure you are buying real fruit juice, reject anything labelled 'fruit juice drink', 'a refreshing combination of six fruit juices', 'island blend', 'nectar' or 'fruit drink', and hold out for the words 'fruit juice'. This signifies real fruit juice, extracted from fruit, and either packed fresh or reconstituted from concentrated juice.

Fruit 'squash' must contain at least 25 per cent juice

(plus added sugar) while a 'drink' needs only 10 per cent fruit juice in it (plus sugar) to qualify for the name.

TECHNOFOOD

After our food is grown and harvested it undergoes another serious onslaught in the food processing industry. It is not only the way that our food is grown but the entire pattern of what we eat and what our children love to eat that has changed radically in the space of a generation.

Highly-processed food, mucked about with chemicals, artificially coloured, flavoured and smartened up, packaged, sometimes cooked and ready for reheating, has taken over from the simple fare that came raw from the market or garden and was cooked in our own kitchens. Processing in itself need not be a bad thing: many women have been liberated from time-consuming cooking at home by modern convenience foods. But, all too often, processing is used as an opportunity to adulterate food, adding synthetic colours and flavours to make it appear to be of a better quality than it actually is. Eighty per cent of the money we spend on food now goes on the processed varieties.

We are eating less fresh fish and meat – but more frozen. We eat half the amount of bread that was consumed a generation ago, and only a third of the porridge – while sales of breakfast cereals have trebled. We buy far fewer potatoes – yet many more frozen chips; while sales of crisps have gone up fivefold in twenty years. The amount of sweets, crisps, biscuits, soft drinks and ice-creams consumed in Britain are worth £8 billion every year. Each person in Britain eats an average of four kilos of preservatives yearly. And we eat more processed food than virtually any other nation in the world.

'Many of the products we buy in the food stores today have never been eaten before. Young, growing children may be particularly vulnerable to these unusual, inappropriate foods and untested chemicals. They could be heading into a whole lot of trouble.'

Tim Lobstein of the London Food Commission in *Children's Food* (Unwin Paperbacks).

For two decades we have known that food additives – like the bright food colourings in soft drinks and sweets – can give children asthma, skin rashes and cause behavioural problems. Some of these have been banned from babies' and young children's food. Yet in *Children's Food*, Tim Lobstein, of the London Food Commission, shows that many common brands of drinks and sweets are still widely sold with these banned dyes and additives. Some give instructions on how to dilute the drinks for babies and young children.

Meanwhile, the value to our health of these kinds of food is being increasingly questioned. The implications for children's health are particularly worrying: children are still growing and are also more vulnerable to infections, pollutants and other long-term health risks. The quality of food eaten by pregnant (and would-be pregnant) women is also important, not only to the mother's health but to the health of her future child.

IN THE MOUTHS OF BABES

The younger the child, the more vulnerable her or his health. And while it has long been agreed that the best food for newborns is their mother's milk, a third of all babies who start off this way stop breastfeeding by the time they are one week old. The longer mothers stay in hospital after birth, the more likely they are to give up breastfeeding and turn to the commercial preparations.

> 'Some cosmetic additives – notably colours and flavours – and some preservatives, certainly can make some vulnerable people ill, and should not be used in food liable to be eaten by babies and young children under five years of age.'
> Geoffrey Cannon, author of *The Politics of Food*, in *Living Earth*, July/September 1988.

An ingredient beloved of children and invariably found in processed snack food is sugar. Sugar is quickly digested and burnt up by the body, providing a 'high' in blood sugar quickly followed by a low (the 'sugar jag') – which in turn demands another sugary snack, and so on. Again, we don't know the long-term effects of this kind of eating but long-term sugar consumption has been linked to diabetes, heart disease, dermatitis and even cancer. There has been a dramatic rise in diabetes in the last two decades.

Baby food manufacturers spend a massive £4 million a year promoting their products – compared to the £$\frac{3}{4}$ million Health Education Council 'Healthy Eating' budget. Tim Lobstein argues not only that the responsible government bodies and the food industry are in bed together, but that the food industry has systematically and cynically manipulated parents' desires to give their children healthy and natural food by making outrageous statements about the purity of their products.

Take some of the claims on food labels. A baby's rusk can carry a 'low sugar' tag – even when it contains more sugar than a doughnut. 'No added sugars' can simply mean that other sweeteners have been used. The claim 'no artificial sweeteners' is entirely meaningless as artificial sweeteners are already banned from baby food.

There also tends to be a lot of aluminium in baby foods – no limits have been set – despite the fact that this metal is implicated in Alzheimer's disease and has been linked to learning problems in children. On the other hand, aluminium in baby food may not be dangerous – but we don't know this for sure.

As for those other children's favourites, fish fingers and sausages, their actual fish and meat content has been gradually dwindling over the years. In a 1983 survey, the

'We can soon have 100 per cent calorie-free sugars, fats and starches, spun and woven into any textures and mixtures we want – and even powdered with vitamins to keep us alive. All this courtesy of your local chemical industry. No one quite knows what problems these "foods" might lead to in the human population. But what the heck – we will find out soon enough! At least, our children will.'
Tim Lobstein in *Children's Food*
(Unwin Paperbacks).

average fish finger was little more than half fish (often in the form of fish mince, soaked in a polyphosphate solution), while some contained as little as one third. The rest was a mixture of water, batter and breadcrumbs.

And processing techniques have destroyed so many of the nutrients in breakfast cereals that vitamins have had to be added to make them worth eating. Iron is added to many cereals – but not in the form found in food like meat or spinach. According to Tim Lobstein, the iron in cereals is just any old iron of the nuts and bolts variety, and it has been claimed that much of it comes as a by-product of the scrap-car industry. The human body can't digest this form of iron very easily, and so ten times as much as we need is added to the cereals to ensure that some will be absorbed. Lobstein reports a rumour that experimental animals lived longer if they ate the packet rather than the cereals!

CHILDREN ARE WHAT THEY EAT

So what are the consequences of our modern, technofood diet? Britain has one of the worst records of diet-related ill health in Europe. The health effects on children cover a range from learning and behavioural problems to asthma, eczema, rashes and hyperactivity.

In the longer term, heart disease – clearly linked with diet – accounts for a quarter of all deaths, and the rate for men dying of heart disease in their thirties and forties has doubled since the war. Some 5,000 people a week die of coronary heart disease in Britain. Estimates vary, but between 35 and 50 per cent of cancers are thought to be food related, especially those of the bowel, breast, uterus and gall-bladder.

So if we already know these grim statistics, why haven't we made changes in our diet? The answer is a political one

'Sir Richard Doll, an eminent medical epidemiologist, has summarized the advice: "Whether the object is to avoid cancer, coronary heart disease, hypertension, diabetes, diverticular disease, duodenal ulcer, or constipation, there is broad agreement among research workers that the type of diet that is least likely to cause disease is one that provides a high proportion of calories in whole grain cereals, vegetables and fruit; provides most of its animal protein in fish and poultry; limits the intake of fats and, if oils are to be used, gives preference to liquid vegetable oils; includes very few dairy products, eggs and little refined sugar." '

From 'This Food Business' prepared by the London Food Commission for the *New Statesman and Society* and Channel Four.

with a shameful government record of inaction and collaboration with the food industry. At the beginning of the 1980s, an important report from N A C N E (the National Advisory Committee on Nutritional Education) spelled out how unhealthy our diet has become. Britons eat too much sugar, salt, saturated fat and additives. We need to eat more fruit and vegetables. But the report was never made public.

The interests of the strong and well-organized food lobby have been put before those of consumers time and again as governments show more interest in shifting the latest sugar or butter mountain than in safeguarding the nation's health. And the government continues to cut

'Many of the lead lines now on sale in our supermarkets appear to be rich in wholegrain cereal, vegetables or fruit, or fresh meat, while in truth they are highly processed products, not fresh and drained of goodness. This is not only legalised consumer fraud, but also amounts to a menace to public health: because it is these products, above all, that are stuffed with hard fats, processed sugars, salt and chemicals. They are counterfeit food.'

Geoffrey Cannon in *Living Earth*,
September 1989.

funding to food safety research centres. The Institute of Food Research in Bristol, which pioneered work on botulism, salmonella and listeria, has been closed down.

A PRICE TAG ON HEALTH

Once consumers are armed with the facts, they have proved keen to change their diets. Already people are eating less processed meat and sugar, and more wholemeal bread, fruit and vegetables. But cost is still a major barrier to a healthier diet, and low-income families are changing their diets more slowly than the affluent.

Good food costs more, and the healthier foods have gone up in price faster than the less-healthy types. Organic foods and hormone-free meat are more expensive than their factory-farmed, mass-produced equivalents. And families struggling to pay fixed bills – like mortgages or fuel bills – can end up spending even less money on food.

In late twentieth-century Britain, particularly under Thatcher, the 'haves', with their credit cards and cars, drive to shop in the big, upmarket supermarkets, while a second tier of consumers has less access to affordable good food. At the bottom of the pile are those who sometimes can't afford to eat at all: the city of Edinburgh has begun a widespread voluntary distribution of food, mostly through its churches.

'As state benefits decrease and the price of food rises in preparation for the completion of the European market in 1992, low-income families are increasingly forced to "trade down" to worse and worse quality food in order to survive. "Diseases of affluence" is a misleading term. The cancers, heart disease and obesity caused by over-consumption of saturated fats, sugar and salt (and underconsumption of fibre) are, in fact, the diseases of the poor in affluent Western societies.'

Alexandra Artley in the *Spectator*,
August 1989.

Parents who can't afford decent, nourishing food for their children find it extremely distressing. An increasing number of homeless and single-parent families are stuck in bed and breakfast accommodation in our towns and cities, without enough money to buy decent food and without cooking facilities to prepare anything nutritional for their children.

MAD, BAD AND DANGEROUS MEAT

In the name of greater productivity and profit, the rearing of animals in Britain has developed into an intensive, 'scientific' industry, far removed from the natural order. Huge factory farms have taken over from the old-style mixed farming on a smaller scale. Britain has led the world in developing methods of intensive animal rearing and research into the forms of animal feed that can be given as a substitute to traditional free-range foraging and pasture.

In the late 1980s, the public learned with disgust that animals were being fed on their own recycled waste. Recycled sheep carcasses were being fed to cows, and chicken excrement and carcasses scraped up as cheap animal protein.

The result? An epidemic of food contamination, with botulism, salmonella and the frightening disease BSE (Bovine Spongiform Encephalopathy), threatened food supplies. In 1988, reported food poisoning cases passed the 40,000 mark – more than double the rate of 1985. And it is thought that between ten and one hundred times as many cases generally go unreported.

Britain is the only country in Europe with the fatal 'mad cow' disease, BSE. In the space of two years, the number of cases of this disease has gone up from three a week to 175 a week in 1990.

BSE first appeared in 1985 and it has affected 2,000 herds of cattle. Although so far the risks seem to be small, there are fears that this fatal form of dementia could be passed from cattle to humans. So far there is no evidence that BSE can infect humans, but it is a disease that can't be detected until several years have passed and much damage to the brain has already been done. The government has now allocated millions to BSE research, but in the meantime, the only sure way to avoid any risk is to avoid British beef.

HAMBURGER HAVOC

Children love them. Parents love the convenience. But sadly, those fast-food hamburgers carry a terrible price tag.

> 'Hamburgers . . . are about the least "local" food that you can possibly buy. If you eat a hamburger in England, for example, the meat may well come from English cattle fed on American maize and soya from Brazil, or even from Thailand. The bun will be baked in England, but the wheat in it will come from North America. The cheese (processed) will be from Holland, the onions from Spain, the tomatoes from Italy and the lettuce from Spain or California. Although the chips will probably be made from local potatoes, the wrapping that encloses them will be made from Scandinavian paper.'
> John Seymour and Herbert Girardet in
> *Blueprint for a Green Planet*
> (Dorling Kindersley).

By 1985, two-thirds of Central America's accessible rainforests had been destroyed in order to feed cattle for western consumption. The forest clearance began in the mid-1960s to make room for cattle ranches. By the mid-1970s, sales of hamburgers were doubling every five years.

By the mid-1980s, 140 hamburgers a second were being bought from one fast-food chain alone.

The multi-national fast-food chains deny that they use beef from Central and South America, but environmentalists say there is no doubt about this 'hamburger connection'. European hamburger meat does come from Europe, but half the soya meal used to fatten the animals up comes from Brazil and other Third World countries. To grow that soya, many small farmers have been dispossessed and forests cleared.

Finally, McDonald's burgers – although promoted with huge advertising campaigns aimed at children – aren't judged to be particularly good for children. In the USA, the Texan Attorney-General ruled, in a court case over advertising claims, that 'McDonald's food is, as a whole, not nutritious'.

What can you do? Give the fast-food burger a wide berth, and turn to good old fish and chips!

SAFE MEAT

The more we hear about meat and how it is produced – with antibiotics, with cruelty, and slaughtered with little regard for hygiene – the less of a good idea it seems. But if you don't want to take your children down the vegetarian path, it's worth shelling out perhaps twice as much money for meat of decent quality, and eating it a little less often. Try some delicious, nutritious and 'green' vegetarian alternatives. Or give game meats like rabbit or wild venison a go, when you can get it. Wild animals are more likely to have lived and died with dignity.

Jack Sprat (who ate no fat) had the right idea: animals store poisons – such as pesticide residues – in their fat in order to keep them away from other vital organs. This is another reason for sticking to lean and well-reared meat. Avoid smoked meats too (or any smoked foods like cheese or kippers), if you are worried about carcinogens (cancer-inducing chemicals) which are imparted by the smoking process.

> 'Intensive production methods throughout the world harm the global environment. They cause water pollution, acid rain, the spread of deserts, and contribute to the greenhouse effect and the loss of tropical forests.'
> From *Living Earth*, April–June 1989.

The Soil Association launched their 'Safe Meat' campaign in 1989, to encourage people to turn to meat that is reared by organic standards – and is therefore nutritious, safe to eat and reared by sustainable and benign methods. Livestock reared to organic standards are fed on organically-grown feedstuffs, cannot be treated with drugs when healthy or given food additives and they are treated humanely. Send for their 'Safe Meat' lists, giving farms on a regional or national basis (£2 or £10 respectively) from the Soil Association, 86–8 Colston Street, Bristol, Avon BS1 5BB.

Alternatively, try the Real Meat Company which provides additive-free meat from humanely-reared animals. They have a shop in Bath, but also sell mail order from The Real Meat Company, East Hill Farm, Heytesbury, Warminster, Wiltshire, BA12 0HR (tel: 0985 40436/40060).

NO MEAT

You and your children don't need to eat meat to stay healthy. In fact, vegetarians claim they are among the healthiest people around, and they can expect to live nine years longer than meat eaters (this is often because heart and circulatory diseases are rarer). These days, almost half the population in Britain is trying to avoid meat, according to a survey by the Food Research Association in January 1990.

Vegetarian food is usually cheaper, and the food you eat uses much less land and energy to produce than meat. Avoiding meat also means avoiding the antibiotics, hormones and pesticides in most mass-produced meat – and avoiding the cruelty to which many farm animals are subjected. But do take care to plan your diet, especially if you are bringing your children up as vegetarians; try *Vegetarian Cooking for Children* by Rosamund Richardson for ideas.

The Vegetarian Society has a very popular and active youth wing, appealing to the million and a half young people (under sixteen) who are choosing to turn their backs on meat. The under-twelves have their own club called The Green Gang. Members get free leaflets (like *Very Easy Veggie Recipes* and *Talk About Factory Farming*), plus badges, stickers and magazines. Membership is £3.50 for anyone under eighteen.

Club VI (Vegetarians First) is for the aged twelve to eighteens, and members get copies of the lively and informative magazine *Greenscene*, plus a membership card which entitles them to discounts at various health food shops, with leaflets, badges and stickers. Their booklet on ideas for campaigning tells you how to go about setting up a vegetarian group at school, while the 'Food

Without Fear' video sets out to deal with all the vital issues surrounding vegetarianism.

For more information about all aspects of vegetarianism contact the society at Parkdale, Dunham Road, Altrincham, Cheshire WA14 4QG (tel: 061 928 0793). There are two school campaigns run by the society as well (see Education).

CHICKEN AND EGG

In Britain, everyone knows that salmonella is rife amongst chickens and their eggs. Edwina Currie was sacked after her initial statement that most egg production is infected with the bug (she later qualified it). Young children, old and unwell people have been advised not to eat eggs.

More than half of chickens on sale are also thought to be contaminated with salmonella, largely because of poor practices at slaughterhouses where machines are not being cleansed after an infected bird has been 'processed'; all the birds that follow down the production line are then infected by the dirty machine.

With chickens, turkeys and eggs, ignore labels like 'farm fresh' and hold out for 'free range' available from good butchers and supermarkets. The Free-Range Egg Association (FREGG) lobbies for more humane egg production. Unfortunately, the Soil Association say that the plans for a new Euro-definition of 'free range' are a 'travesty'. For more information, contact the Soil Association or FREGG, 37 Tanza Road, London, NW3 2UA (tel: 071 435 2596). Or why not try keeping half a dozen chickens of your own if you have a garden? The average garden is quite large enough, and the hens will eat up all your kitchen waste while providing you with delicious fresh eggs.

LISTERIOSIS

Listeriosis, a particularly dangerous form of food poisoning, is also on the increase. Not much is known about the onset of this disease, but it is associated with being in an 'immunocompromised' state – such as pregnancy. It can kill one in four victims and can damage or kill the unborn child. According to the London Food Commission, of 115 cases of listeriosis in pregnant women in England, there were eleven miscarriages, nine stillbirths and six neonatal deaths.

In its report of January 1990, the House of Commons Social Services Select Committee said that pregnant women still face an unnecessary risk of losing their babies from listeria infection. This all-party committee of MPs decided that women may be at risk from listeria in the earliest weeks of pregnancy and should avoid soft cheeses and other suspect foods when trying to conceive.

'According to the London Food Commission, listeria has been found in a wide range of foods, including cheeses, dairy products and vegetables. Tests have revealed listeria in four out of sixty pre-packed salads, sixteen out of sixty-four cook-chill convenience meals, three out of five fresh [raw] chickens and three out of thirty-one chicken pre-cooked meals.'
From *The Food Magazine*, Summer 1989.

The largest survey of listeria so far carried out (in September 1989) showed that one in thirteen samples of cook-chill food are contaminated by the bug. Sandwiches, custard and cream-filled confectionary as well as other ready-to-eat food were infected. There are also concerns that inadequate cooking instructions on prepared food – particularly for microwaves – have contributed to the listeria and salmonella poisoning epidemic.

A PROCESS OF PERFECTION?

A new and potentially sinister method of making food seem healthier than it really is, is irradiation. This process bombards food with gamma rays from a radioactive source to change its chemical structure. It has been declared safe by the World Health Organisation, and as part of the Food Safety Bill the government is lifting a twenty-year ban to use it on food (it has previously been used on sterilizing medical equipment).

Food irradiation can make fruit and vegetables last longer. It can stop potatoes from sprouting and it does kill most bacteria and bugs in raw food – like salmonella.

But on the BBC's programme 'This Week' in February 1990, Professor Richard Lacey, an eminent microbiologist from Leeds University, produced evidence that irradiation did not kill listeria which had been injected into chicken. And when that chicken was stored in a chill cabinet, the listeria increased.

Irradiation also means that you won't be able to trust your nose any longer. This method kills food poisoning bacteria that can give off a bad smell – yet the toxins (made by the bacteria) that cause illness are left unaffected.

The risk is that manufacturers will use irradiation to cover up the flaws in food – like those caused by poor hygiene or the bacteria found when food is going off. Irradiation also damages important nutrients in food, such as vitamins, and we simply don't know what its effect will be in combination with pesticide residues.

Not only are about 80 per cent of consumers against food irradiation but groups as diverse as the British Medical Association, the Women's Institutes, the Consumers' Association, the farmers' unions, the Retail Consortium and the Institute of Environmental Health Officers have come out against it. Yet the government and the EEC have decided that we shall have it.

The Food Irradiation Campaign predicts the scheme will do for a whole spectrum of foodstuffs what Edwina Currie did for eggs. Because if food needs to be irradiated, consumers will want to know what's wrong with it. If you are interested in obtaining more information, contact Tony Webb, Food Irradiation Campaign, London Food Commission, 88 Old Street, London EC1V 9AR (tel: 071 253 9513).

UNDERCOVER DANGERS

Plastic cling film is made with chemicals called plasticizers that can 'migrate' into food. Platicizers can cause cancer. The fattier the food, the faster the plasticizers are absorbed.

So try to avoid plastic film, particularly on fatty foods like cheese and meats. Use greaseproof paper instead: it's less polluting too. If you must use plastic film, try using it to cover bowls of food so that it doesn't come into contact with the food itself. Or try non-toxic cling film from the mail order service Foodwatch International, at Butts Pond Industrial Estate, Sturminster Newton, Dorset DT10 1AZ (tel: 0258 73356).

NOT FOR THE CHILDREN

They're not good for children (with their stimulant and addictive drug effects) and they're not good for us, but most parents would rather live with a double standard than do without those necessary reviving cups of tea or coffee.

But if you want to feel better about your bad habits, beware of which brands you buy. It's well established that the production of tea and coffee (and they're not the only ones) bring poverty to both the land and people of the Third World. In some tea-producing countries, children work on the plantations as virtual slaves. Tea workers almost everywhere work for appallingly low wages and generally have to live in overcrowded and unhealthy conditions.

Instant coffee is not only often produced under conditions of exploitation, but it is hugely expensive to produce in terms of energy. The roasting, grinding and processing make it ten times as energy extravagant as a fish finger and a hundred times more so than ice.

But there are various organisations – like Oxfam and Traidcraft – which now sell tea and coffee (as well as other products) on a 'fair trade' basis. Traidcraft is a company which was started to provide an alternative way of trading with the Third World by setting up just, direct links with the people who make the goods. Their aim is international justice, no less, and they work with a wide variety of aid organisations. It has rapidly blossomed and now it sells a wide range of teas and coffees through its local representatives and shops at prices only slightly higher than the supermarket brands. Contact Traidcraft plc, Kingsway, Gateshead, Tyne and Wear NE11 0NE (tel: 091 487 3191).

BIG SHOPS

When you've got a family to feed, it's hard to beat the convenience of a big supermarket where everything is sold under the same roof. And encouragingly, since the late 1980s, the big supermarkets have been tripping over each other in the rush to be seen to be green. Organic produce is appearing on their shelves together with leaflets detailing how environmentally friendly they are.

'If 10 per cent of the customers for a product change their minds, or demand a change in the nature of that product, then the supplier will think very hard about changing or withdrawing it.'
John Button in *Green Pages* (Optima).

John Button, of *Green Pages*, sent a questionnaire to the leading supermarket chains, asking them to describe their attitudes to food additives, labelling, organic food, South Africa and educational literature. He concluded that Safeway was a close contender for the 'most aware supermarket' award, having introduced organic produce to all of its 125 outlets, and having removed fifty of the fifty-seven most dangerous food additives from their own-label products. The Co-Op, with its ban on South African goods, and its commitment to food labelling and consumer education, was John Button's winner however. Sainsbury's also scored highly, with Tesco and Waitrose doing well on healthier eating. But several high street chains got the thumbs down for their performance on most of these issues, although changes are being rapidly made.

SMALL SHOPS

At the other end of the spectrum from the supermarkets – which are often owned by multinational food companies – are the wholefood shops. These are often independent co-operatives run by people with a commitment to change. It is here that parents will find the kind of additive-free and organic food that is best for children's health.

Wholefood shops are no longer the stamping ground of the lentil-eating classes. Now, almost every town and many a village has a shop – or at least some shelves of a shop – stocked with pulses, beans and muesli. More and more are stocking organic produce too.

If you want to track down the best shops near you, enquire with your local environmental group – like Friends of the Earth – if anyone has done a *Green Pages* for your area. These strictly local directories are an excellent source of information. Or, for a sampling of what's available nationally, dip into John Button's *Green Guide to England* which is published by Green Print.

FOODWATCH

Alternatively try the mail order Foodwatch International service which supplies a wide range of organically-produced and additive-free foodstuffs. Foodwatch is particularly useful for people suffering from allergies, and its lines include plenty of additive-free treats for children – like natural jelly, mousse, or burger mixes. Foodwatch also sell non-toxic cling film and Ecover detergents. Inevitably, it costs more than the supermarket. It can be found at Butts Pond Industrial Estate, Sturminster Newton, Dorset DT10 1AZ (tel: 0258 73356).

Food For Free

You don't have to buy all of your food. Why not try:

- **Home growing.** In even a small garden room can be made for a few vegetables, salads or herbs. Or why not think about working an allotment like nearly half a million other Britons. On the smallest scale, pots of parsley, chives, basil and other herbs can thrive on your windowsill, while seeds and beans can be sprouted in jam jars.
- **Food for Free.** As Richard Mabey shows in his book of the same name, the countryside has a wealth of wild, edible plants just there for the plucking. But never eat anything you can't positively identify as safe, and take care not to pick more than you need.
- If you want to grow some of your own food, the Henry Doubleday Research Association for organic gardeners has its own information service as well as a wide-ranging mail order service.

3

Play

Childhood is a precious time – a time of intense experience, of fresh imagination, of dedicated play. Play takes up much of a child's life, and as parents we can help children towards the kind of play which will satisfy and enrich them. For what children learn today will shape the sort of world they create tomorrow.

> 'Good though some toys are, most toys simply add to the mountain of consumer goods which are overpackaged, use large amounts of energy and non-renewable resources in their manufacture, and rapidly become so much non-recycled rubbish.'
> John Button in *Green Pages* (Optima).

To watch children playing – and to play with them – as they develop from babyhood, through toddlerhood and into school, is a fascinating experience. All parents know how avidly a small baby will watch running water, smoke from a bonfire, or leaves fluttering in the park. Indoors, a mobile or bright pictures can have the same effect.

Once they are old enough to grasp and bash objects about, babies do so with deep concentration. As toddlers, they get to grips with the physical world with the greatest intensity: touching everything, poking fingers in and getting hold of anything in their reach. Before long – perhaps at a mother and toddler group or simply with the children of friends and neighbours – they are learning how to play and share with others of their own size. At first there is a certain amount of push and shove and toddlers have a breathtaking capacity to behave like little beasts, but most children seem to have a tremendous need for other children's company.

'The ability to develop close relationships in later life is linked to childhood friendships. Some studies suggest that other children are even more important than the mother in a child's emotional development . . . I suspect an over-dependence on toys has a lot to do with not having enough companionship.'
    Karen Christensen in *Home Ecology*
    (Arlington Books).

So, whatever the child psychologists say about play – and they say a great deal – as parents we already know that this is an absolutely fundamental part of every child's life. When children are happy in play they are totally absorbed. Boredom – the fuel of obnoxious behaviour – is kept at bay. Life is rich, amusing and satisfying.

It follows that the kinds of play and playthings our children take up have a vital role in their development. The links between play and early learning are now well understood, but the significance of play to lifelong attitudes and behaviour is surely just as important. If we want our children to develop love and respect for each other, for themselves and for the planet, it is worth taking a closer look at how they spend their play time.

OUTWARD BOUND

Many of the most enduring games which children play don't require any ready-made toys at all. Children are naturally imaginative and have an unquenchable inborn ability to create their own games and fantasies. Just watch them on one of those bleak squares of tarmac known as the school 'playground': like a flock of excited birds they rush about, grouping and regrouping, deeply involved in games of their own making. The old favourites of 'catch', skipping and hand-clapping games are also still very much in currency.

'There is increasing evidence to show that adults are better tempered and less likely to be depressed and miserable when they have plenty of exercise, and children are probably no different.'

Drs Andrew and Penny Stanway in
The Baby and Child Book (Pan Books).

They love to play out of doors – as long as they've got other children to play with and a decent, safe play space. Unfortunately, the dangers of road traffic, and the fear of adults who might harm children, have made it increasingly difficult for children to go off on their bikes or down to the playground without an adult in tow.

There is increasing pressure on community play spaces these days because of the sale of land for development. According to the National Playing Fields Association, in 1990, 800 sites are at risk. But, at the same time, there are signs of more creative thinking about what kind of play spaces children actually need, particularly, of course, in urban areas.

'Rosy Martin [of the Women's Design Service] welcomes new initiatives, such as community gardens, as an example of the way in which play is seen as more than a mere decanting of excess energy on the climbing frame. "Wild" areas, with a butterfly garden or a section of unmowed grassland, can be incorporated into urban and rural play spaces. She adds, "If plants are chosen carefully, you can encourage small animals and insects to use the play space." '

From the *Guardian*, January 1990.

TOYS, TOYS, TOYS ...

There is a role for ready-made toys for indoor play. The childcare guru Penelope Leach argues that in our modern,

mostly urban world, small children can take years to find
out how the world really works. Western children no
longer go with their parents to work in the fields, growing
up with an understanding of nature. How are they to
know that milk comes from cows, not bottles, or that
concrete and tarmac are not the natural skin of the planet?

Toys, argues Leach, can enable children to learn about
the world as well as giving them possessions of their own
when parents' toys (stereos, cars, and telephones) are
forbidden territory. But the kinds of toys your children
play with can convey a whole host of attitudes and values.
If your child has a cupboard full of plastic, battery-driven
objects which break and get thrown away with alarming
speed, how will she or he understand that we need to
conserve energy and avoid waste? Far better to spend a bit
more on a few less toys, which are durable and well made.
Hand-made and wooden toys are expensive, but they will
last. And they carry their own aesthetic lesson.

BATTERY OF PROBLEMS

Even the new, improved 'green' batteries still fall
very short of being ecologically sound. Batteries
are extremely energy inefficient: the manufacture
of a battery uses up to fifty times more energy
than a battery will ever give out. And once they
are thrown away they become lumps of non-biodegradable metal which add to our growing waste
mountain.

There is the question of imagination too. Whose vision,
whose fantasy is the child drawn into when she plays with
a little pink plastic pony? Not her own in the first instance

surely – although she may build new imaginings on the beloved object.

There is a lot more to be said for the long-established staples of play – like sand, water, dough, paints and crayons, pots and pans, bricks and balls – than for much of the highly-expensive, highly-packaged dross that gets its allure from television.

Any parent who has put in time at Playgroup knows that children can learn a wide range of skills and be kept amused for hours in making their own 'toys'. Those toilet rolls and cereal boxes held together by gallons of glue and decorated with soggy crêpe paper and split peas may look like an unwieldy mess to an adult, but it is a precious combine harvester or steam train to the infant.

It is worth joining a Toy Library if there is one in your area. Contact the Toy Libraries Association at Seabrook House, Wyllyotts Manor, Darkes Lane, Potters Bar, Herts EN6 2HL, for the address of your nearest group and for publications and advice on setting up your own. Or try swapping toys with friends – if your children haven't already done so. Recycle paper and cardboard in your children's direction too: they love cutting out and sticking pictures from old magazines and catalogues, and sending 'letters' in your old envelopes.

WAR!

And then there is the whole category of toys that so many parents dislike – but so many children adore: guns, tanks, fighter aircraft, warships, swords, daggers and soldiers – you name it, adults make it to sell to children (or parents). Is it worth putting up some passive resistance to the onslaught – or is it true that children will play 'bang, bang, you're dead' whether you like it or not?

Surely parents must be guided by their own feelings on this one. If the sight of serried ranks of military advancing across your kitchen floor does not fill you with delight, why should you put up with it? If you feel that there is something wrong when small children play at killing as if it is ordinary fun, why should you bite your tongue?

Perhaps they don't understand what it is they are playing? Well, perhaps now is also the time to tell them you don't really like it and explain why. Few parents put up with any kind of verbal violence, even when children don't understand what it means. Parents will stop children from using 'bad language' because such language is widely considered shocking and aggressive from children. So why should we condone its play equivalent? If, in adult life, we believe that communication, negotiation, reason and compromise are the right way to deal with people who disagree with us, why should we approve of our children eliminating baddies with a hail of imaginary bullets?

It is impossible to stop children playing bang-bang games altogether; they will pick them up from friends and at school; and the business of working through aggressive feelings is a natural part of children's play – as is an intense interest in death. But that doesn't mean we have to buy them toys which are specifically designed for that purpose. Children will point sticks, pencils or their fingers as if they are guns. But when that game is over, the stick, pencil and finger are used for other things. The gun, however, just remains a gun. There is no other way to play with it.

The International Association for the Child's Right to Play (IPA) have taken a stand against war toys and games of violence and destruction. They argue that war toys increase aggressive behaviour, rather than developing more caring and co-operative play. War toys, say the IPA, also give children a sense of power from being destructive, so that destructiveness becomes valued behaviour.

In 1987, Finland became the first country to ban the sale of toys which resemble offensive military weaponry. There is no reason – apart from the loss to manufacturers' profits – why we should not follow suit.

'The property which all war toys and the related harmful toys had in common was that they conveyed to young children contempt for life and a negation of life at the very age when they are most vigorous, inquisitive, trusting and impressionable. Children's play and materials should affirm life and assist children in asserting their natural caring and positive qualities.'

From Scrapstore *Newsletter*, 1988.

Ultimately, it is up to us as parents to pass on our values to our children. Through play our children have the opportunity to learn co-operation, sharing and respect for others. Even as they biff each other over the head with wooden spoons, and grab each others' toys, we have the chance to teach them something about peace. Each time they gather up shells from the beach or conkers from the park they encounter the wonder of the natural world. If we encourage them to play in a tree house or plant their own small garden – rather than play with war toys – perhaps we will help them develop some respect for life in all its forms.

And, in a world which so often seems on the brink of destruction from real, grown-up war, and at risk of devastation from real, grown-up indifference to the environment, we need our children to know better than we did.

The War Toys Campaign is run by a group of people in Cheltenham who urge us all to think before buying war toys. Contact WTC at 50 Union Street, Fairview, Cheltenham, Gloucestershire (tel: 0242 574795).

The Peace Pledge Union also opposes the sale of war toys, and has a Young Peacemakers' Club, with its own monthly newspaper to involve younger children. You can find them at 6 Endsleigh Street, London WC1H 0DX (tel: 071 387 5501).

PLAY FOR LIFE

Have you ever gone around a toyshop looking for something to give a child and come away depressed, dissatisfied and disappointed? Did you see the shelves loaded with plastic warlords, intricately-packaged battery toys and other expensive, easily breakable junk?

Then perhaps you should contact the national voluntary organisation, Play For Life. This group (its founding sponsors include the Green Party, the Peace Pledge Union, Quaker Peace and Service and Traidcraft) sets out to provide playthings which are 'life-affirming', which inspire in children a love of all life and positive responses to their fellow human beings.

The organisation looks for non-sexist and non-racist toys, games and hobbies which help children to develop a

Play Safe

- Yet another good reason for avoiding plastic bags is the risk of suffocation to small children.
- Lead in painted toys may still be a hazard with some imported toys. Check with your local Trading Standards Officer.
- Keep a close eye on children when they get into model making. Solvents and glues are potentially dangerous chemicals.
- Choose non-toxic chalks and crayons rather than felt tips – which are made up of solvents and plastics.
- Watch out for small and/or sharp bits that may come off toys – especially with children under two who put everything in their mouths.
- Don't let them run around with whistles in their mouths, or with toys with sharp corners and edges: a fall on such objects can have awful consequences.

love of life through the opportunities they provide for fun, imagination, wonder, adventure, co-operation and new skills. You can get hold of them through Play For Life's free mail order catalogue (send a large self-addressed envelope plus stamp for up to 100 grams) from Play For Life, 31b Ipswich Road, Norwich NR2 2LN (tel: 0603 505947). Their playthings are for children from three to teenage, and most cost less than £5. They include activity toys (such as balsa wood gliders or a circular swing), musical toys (drums, cimbalas and lyres), puzzles, table games, ethnic and male and female dolls, soft toys and puppets, craft kits and weaving looms, wooden animals and trees, bricks, houses – and much more.

Play For Life believe that through creative play we can help children develop a resourceful and caring outlook so that they will be better able to withstand the pressures and exposure to violence which are so much a part of modern life. Their ambition, no less, is to prepare today's children for 'One World Tomorrow'.

'Good play nourishes the inner being. It provides fun and challenge, new interests and skills, a sense of wonder . . . food for the imagination. It involves contact with the physical world and with nature. It inspires a love of life and encourages the building of new relationships with the self and other people . . . We need to be aware however that not all play is beneficial. There are many toys, games and entertainments as well as social and commercial pressures which exert a damaging influence on children's social development.'
From the Play For Life mail order catalogue.

Play For Life not only makes toys available, it cultivates links with toy manufacturers, it provides resource material and information, it mounts exhibitions, gives talks and workshops, holds conferences and publishes a newsletter. Get in touch with them for more information.

Pandora's Toybox?

What should parents look out for when choosing children's toys? Play For Life have worked out their own detailed checklist for what makes a 'life affirming' plaything, but here are some basic ideas to bear in mind next time you make a foray to the toyship.

Choose toys which encourage, develop or provide:

- joy
- an understanding of other people
- a love of nature and appreciation of the Earth
- creative outlets
- a challenge or puzzle to get to grips with
- opportunities to share, communicate and co-operate
- high aesthetic and design standards.

TOY TIPS

- Don't give too many toys. Children can only play with a few toys at a time, so don't overload them. Put away unused toys for a while. Apart from avoiding the awful chaos of toy bits and pieces all jumbled together, toys brought down from the shelf after a few weeks in hiding will have added novelty value.
- Your child doesn't need to own all the toys on the market personally. There will be plenty of opportunities to play with a wide range of toys at friends'

houses, playgroup or toddlers' group These too will be new and exciting.

- Don't waste your resources on consuming expensive or elaborately-packaged toys which won't be used. Consult your friends around Christmas and birthday times to find out which toys have been most successful with their children. Complicated toys can frustrate and bore small children very quicky, while the simplest ones (like bricks, playdough) provide limitless fuel for the imagination.

- Organisations like Greenpeace, Traidcraft, the Royal Society for the Protection of Birds and the World Wildlife Fund now have a limited range of toys in their mail order catalogues.

> 'There are two main things to remember when it comes to buying things for your baby. The first, and most obvious, is that you will constantly be under pressure to buy more than you need. The second is that since babies can't spend money themselves, the companies who make baby products have to resort to the ploy of making you believe that what they make is absolutely vital to your baby's health, well-being and safety.'
>
> John Button in *Green Pages* (Optima).

'FREE' TOYS

In our advertising-led, consumer society it is sometimes hard to remember that shopping for our children does not necessarily mean loving our children.

Children, of course, are also pretty quick to scent an advantage and it's hard to answer a child who wants such and such battery-driven toy because all of his friends have got one.

But there are innumerable toys you can provide for younger children without going anywhere near a shop. Small children are fascinated by many things which adults find ordinary or mundane. A tin pan becomes a hat, a dishcloth becomes a doll's sleeping bag, wooden spoons become practically anything . . .

- Make dens and 'tents' out of old curtains and bed-spreads arranged across chairs.
- Use large cardboard boxes to make houses for dolls, animals – or even small children.
- A drawer full of scraps – ribbons, cotton reels, cloth, wool, string, corks, cardboard – is a goldmine to any child who has been encouraged to make things.
- Before you send your old kimonos, stack-heeled shoes and kaftans to Oxfam or the jumble sale, consider whether they wouldn't make good dressing-up material. A box full of weird clothes can be an endless source of fantasy and entertainment.
- Provide toddlers with their own cloth or dustpan when you eventually get around to some housework. They might slow you down a bit but small children love to help in whatever you are doing.
- Imaginative games – like 'going shopping', 'going on holiday', 'doctors' or 'school' – don't need any props that you don't already have around the house.
- As long as you've got glue (there's always flour and water paste) and a blunt-ended pair of scissors, almost anything you've got in the house – from old magazines to pasta and lentils – can be stuck onto pieces of paper as art.

- Playdough doesn't have to be bought in plastic containers: make it at home from flour, salt and water (gradually add water to plain or self-raising flour and salt, or bring to the boil in a saucepan equal quantities of cornflour, salt and water – the more stirring and kneading the better).
- Children love cooking. Let them mix, stir, roll pastry and – when they're older – peel and chop fruit and vegetables with you.

MARY, MARY, QUITE CONTRARY
HOW DOES YOUR GARDEN GROW?

There can be few forms of play (for adults as well as children) which are as satisfying, healthy and therapeutic as gardening, and you don't have to own acres of green lawn, or even a backyard, to garden with children.

Planting that first bean seed in a plastic cup at Playgroup and watching it grow can prompt the kind of Life And Death questions from your child that you may well have given up wondering about yourself. And small children also love to help parents – putting leaves in the wheelbarrow, digging the earth, watering plants, sweeping the patio, picking fruit and vegetables.

But why not – if you have the space – give the children their own plot of ground to cultivate? Depending on the age of the child you may have to give quite a lot of help. Preparing the ground takes time without yielding instant results, and young or impatient ones may well give up too soon if they are left to their own devices.

Garden tools can be too big and too sharp to handle without supervision. But avoid the dinky forks and trowels which are sold commercially as children's garden tools: these are usually of very poor quality and they bend and break easily. Let them use the standard size in the small tools, and if they want to do their own digging, hoeing or raking, try cutting down long handles or making shorter ones.

As for choosing what to grow, you can buy packets of flower seeds designed specifically for children, but they are more expensive than other packets. Aim for plants with good, dramatic effects – like runner beans that grow very quickly or sunflowers which are also tall and striking. Nasturtiums are not only fast-growing, practically indestructible and pretty, but the flowers are very tasty in salads too. Bulbs are generally easy to plant and easy to grow.

GARDENS IN MINIATURE

If you haven't got your own garden – or if it's too cold or wet for children to be cultivating their own plot outside – there are other absorbing ways to make a mini garden grow.

- **Garden on a plate.** Many a village child will have taken one of these to the local flower show, but there's no reason for town children not to have the same kind of fun. Simply provide basic materials like moss, a cup full of earth, twigs, leaves, tiny flowers, and shells. A small dish of water (or circle of silver foil) makes a pond, and add some toy farm animals perhaps. With materials like these children can create their own garden on a dinner plate, small tray or biscuit-tin lid.
- **Vegetable tops garden.** Next time you are preparing carrots, potatoes or turnips, give the tops to your child to place in a shallow dish of water. Leave on a

windowsill and wait for the green and feathery fronds to grow . . .

- **Garden in a bottle.** From your recycling collection of glass bottles, find one with a wide body. Wash and thoroughly dry it and pour in a layer of charcoal chips through a paper funnel. Then add potting compost until the bottle is about a third full. Using long narrow implements – chopsticks, perhaps – dig a small planting hole, then lower your plants into it. Press the roots firmly down with your long implement and trickle in water down the side of the glass. If there is a cork or screw top, seal the bottle to keep in moisture, and place it in a sunny spot.
- **Mustard and cress.** Fill an egg box with damp cotton wool or blotting paper and add your seeds.
- **Tomatoes.** These can be grown in a commercial or home-made 'grobag', placed in a sheltered, sunny porch, yard or balcony.

LEAF AND BARK RUBBING

Provide the children with strong white paper, soft lead pencils or soft dark crayons. In the garden or on a walk all they need to do is lay the paper against a tree trunk, hold it still and rub over the paper with the pencil or crayon. Each variety of tree will yield a different pattern. Bring a variety of leaves home, lay them on the table or floor, cover with paper and rub. If you want to make the 'negative' image of your leaves, lay them on top of the paper and splatter paint around them with a paintbrush or toothbrush.

- **Seeds and beans.** Try sprouting alfalfa and mung beans. You can do this in a jam jar, or send for the 'Gro Ball' from Youth Tag (the Intermediate Technology Youth group). This is a complete sprouting kit with seeds, instructions and recipes. Send £3.50 to IT Publications Ltd, 103–5 Southampton Road, London WC1B 4HH.

GREEN READING FOR CHILDREN

Although there has been an explosion of green books for adults in recent years, parents are still complaining that it's hard to find books for children with a green message.

The annual Earthworm Award is helping to change all that. This is the first 'green' children's book prize, set up to promote and reward environmental awareness and sensitivity in literature for children of all ages. The judges (in 1989 they included *The Snowman* author Raymond Briggs and journalist Michael Buerk) look for books that not only highlight the threats to our natural world but also celebrate and explore its richness, variety and beauty.

Books For A Change at 52 Charing Cross Rd, London WC2H 0BB, is a major stockist of green books, or try Green Books, Ford House, Hartland, Bideford, Devon EX39 6EE (tel: 0237 44621). There are lots of ideas in the Education chapter too.

But good reading doesn't necessarily mean books. Newly launched in 1990 is a bright, lively mag for four to eight year olds called *Play And Learn for Tomorrow's World*. The theme of its first issue was 'Our Rainforests', and after an introduction by Gerald Durrell it provided twenty-eight pages of projects, stories, puzzles and games. It manages to be entertaining and not in the least bit patronizing – and the fact that the magazine is also very instructive (it will be an eye-opener to many parents too) seems like just an added bonus. There is a simple experiment to show how plants make water, a game of glueing rainforest 'cards' onto a world map, a cut-out parrot mobile and plenty of scope for colouring in, finding animals hidden in the forest, and much more. The magazine is obtainable from Play and Learn, 36 High Street, Saxmundham, Suffolk IP17 1AB, and it costs £1.50.

GAMES FOR LAUGHS

Games don't always have to have winners and losers. True, it's a hard world that our children will grow into and competitive games may make them prepared. But isn't it worth teaching them about co-operation and sharing too?

Some games and activities that should leave no child feeling like a failure include:

- **Affirmations:** each person in a circle writes their name on a piece of paper which is folded down and passed around for all the others in turn to write something nice about that person. At the end, you get your own paper back, read the comments – and glow . . . !
- **Procession:** two rows of people join hands to carry a friend around the room on the cradle of their arms – or above their heads if they are strong enough.
- **The old favourites:** Hide and Seek, Blind Man's Buff, Pass the Parcel (where everyone gets a treat at each unwrapping), Grandmother's Footsteps and Consequences (drawing or writing) have much to recommend them as games which put nobody 'out'.

Play For Life also produce a handbook called *Winners All* (which costs £1) with some fifty co-operative games for children and adult groups or parties. And the publishers Green Print have produced a new book by Mildred Masheder called *Let's Play Together* (£4.99) which also describes many co-operative games for all ages.

RECYCLED PLAY

One scheme which combines the best of play opportunities with a national recycling scheme is the Children's Scrapstore.

Scrapstores are resource centres for children which collect all sorts of interesting left-overs from local businesses, public bodies and industry. These 'scraps' can be used as play materials by children's groups, playgroups, local nurseries, youth clubs, adventure playgrounds, schools – or any group providing care, educational or play facilities for children or the disabled. Children benefit from the many play materials they would not otherwise have been able to use (or afford), while local companies cut their waste disposal costs and improve their standing in the community.

Set up in 1980 by the Federation of Resource Centres, there are now more than thirty scrapstores across the country. Scrapstore also has various items which members can rent for a reasonable charge – including marquees, trampettes, crawl tunnels, badgemaker, minibus and more. Members are also entitled to a range of services, from art and craft materials, workshops and training, to the information library and newsletter. Contact the Federation of Resource Centres, Greater Manchester Play Resource Unit, Grumpy House, Vaughan Street, West Gorton, Manchester M12 5DU (tel: 061 223 9730) for more information.

Scrapstore also runs the Scrapstore Camp in beautiful Pembrokeshire which is open to groups, families and

'The South London Children's Scrapstore supplies play materials to more than 35,000 children in south London, gathering the waste from about 150 local manufacturers and retailers, and from other scrapstores. The SLCSS holds regular workshop demonstrations on how to use waste materials as playthings, is represented at many local events and festivals and produces the Scrap and Scratch Opera.'
From *Recycling: a guide for local groups*,
Shell Better Britain Campaign.

individuals of any age. You can put a tent up or stay in their holiday cottage (the ground floor is designed with wheelchair users in mind) or gypsy caravan. The camp has four acres of woodland, stream and pond, and a small river with bathing spots. Telephone 0239 77670 for more information.

SQUARE EYES SYNDROME

While there are some very good programmes for children on television (and recently a spate of programmes about recycling, animal survival and the environment) it is all too easy to let television become a substitute for play.

Too much tv numbs the mind, leaving the whole family staring like mesmerized rabbits as one advert after another fills their heads with the desire to consume. Do we really want to follow so hard on the heels of American culture? In the USA, the average consumer is bombarded with some 5,000 advertising messages a day.

What about the violence that permeates so much of television? According to a conference of the International Association for the Child's Right to Play in 1986, pre-school children who were exposed to violent television for two weeks would push, shove, kick, choke and hit each other at three times their previous rate.

Television may also be implicated in the dramatic rise in suicides of children under ten. According to a report from the World Health Organisation, young children see television actors die and reappear in other programmes so often that they don't see death as something permanent. Suicide is the second highest killer of children between fifteen and twenty-four in the USA.

There are also serious environmental drawbacks to television. So the next time the children tune into 'Neighbours' (or are you an addict too?) why not hit them with a few facts. For instance, every year the electricity used by Britain's televisions produces

- 7 million tonnes of carbon dioxide
- 10,000 tons of sulphur dioxide
- 18,500 tonnes of nitrogen oxides
- 830 cubic metres of radioactive waste.

So switch it off and take them all outside . . .

4

Education

* conventional education * green ideas
* green teaching * 'deep green' teaching * drama
* Centre for Alternative Technology * playgroups
* small schools * alternatives to school
* the Commonwork Centre * Third World links
* parents taking part * projects *

No one who lives in Britain can have failed to notice that education (of the traditional kind) is in crisis. Schools say they are short of funds – and short of teachers. Teachers say they are short of a decent salary and low in morale. And children?

Children don't really have a say. That does not seem to be the point of modern education. The structure of our competitive, exam-based system serves to emphasize training for jobs, not 'woolly liberal' notions like teaching children to think for themselves or helping them to fulfil their potential. It is to the eternal credit of individual teachers – given the obstacles they face – that some of them do manage to instil a genuine sense of self-worth in children, and an enthusiasm for learning.

Implicit in the way that we educate our children is the

> 'If we wish to create a lasting peace, if we want to fight a war against war, we have to begin with the children.' Mahatma Gandhi

so-called 'hidden curriculum'. In other words, much of the impact which school has on our children comes from the style and the environment of their education. School is a place of hierarchies: it is undemocratic and authoritarian; what teacher says, goes. And just as school encourages conformity in our society, it also tends to reflect and reinforce the sexist and racist values around us.

> 'Traditionally, education has been designed to serve those in power, to inculcate acceptance of that power in the young and to prepare people for their 'proper' station in life ... Against this is the possibility that, one day, we may be able to live our own lives, having sufficient self-knowledge, without having to be told what to think and do by someone who claims to "know better", to live in harmony with our communities and our planet.'
> Paul Butler in *Routes to Change*,
> Green Party Education Working Group.

Accordingly, as children learn that they will be rewarded for obedience and conformity, so they learn to accept hierarchy. As they learn to glean information from books, so they learn to believe 'expert' opinion to be more valid than their own. And as the pressure to pass exams in order to get the 'best' jobs mounts, so they learn that the most valued prize of future life is material 'success'.

OPENING EDUCATION

While there is a lot of dissatisfaction with education today, there is also a tremendous surge of new ideas and the whiff of change in the air. Of course, the debate about what good education means, what it is really for, has been raging for centuries. Modern thinkers from Rousseau onwards have joined the argument about how we should bring up our children. Should we give them freedom to develop their inborn creativity, to develop their individuality with a wide range of educational opportunities? Or should we concentrate on a disciplined approach, making sure they learn useful skills and leave school equipped to take part in the world of work? Or, can these various aims be reconciled in one system of education?

Much of the best of modern education today is indebted to the progressive educators of the last 200 years. Amongst them are Friedrich Froebel (1782–1852) who evolved a new educational system which was co-operative and geared to providing for different stages of child development. He coined the name 'Kindergarten' and promoted fantasy and play in education. Rudolph Steiner (1861–1925) was responsible for developing a new school in Stuttgart. He believed that education should help in the unfolding of each child's particular 'spiritual essence' and individual gifts. A string of 'Steiner' (or Waldorf) schools in Europe, America and Britain have followed his ideas.

Another well-known pioneer in progressive education is Maria Montessori who set up her 'House of Childhood' in the slums of Rome. Montessori developed a style of education which took its lead from the needs of the individual child. Instead of imposing a set curriculum upon children, the idea was to allow children to learn through activities appropriate to the stage of each child's development. There are now many Montessori schools worldwide.

GREEN TEACHERS

In many respects these educators are the spiritual forebears of today's 'green teachers' and their thinking belongs to what is now known as the 'holistic' philosophy of education, educating the 'whole' child in mind, body and spirit.

Damian Randle, editor of *Green Teacher* magazine and author of *Teaching Green*, has been at the hub of the holistic education movement in Britain for some time. In his book he describes how people concerned with green matters usually start at the 'shallow' level – how to clean up our rivers, protect the ozone level and so on. But if they carry on thinking about these issues, it leads to a much 'deeper' level of thinking where we have to tackle our basic assumptions about how to be in the world.

Green teachers like Randle are arguing that the most basic common assumptions of our culture must be re-examined. For too long we have accepted that 'Man' conquers nature, exploits the earth for gain and dominates and exploits other men and all women. A new model of co-operation and sensitivity to the earth is urgently needed. And the deeper people follow these ideas, the deeper the desire for 'holism' – a sense of wholeness – becomes.

In green education today, a whole spectrum of new initiatives and ideas, from the shallowest to the deepest, is

'When we know how all the elements of the ecosystem are linked together, we cannot, as happens today, then mistreat one part and hope that others are unaffected. When we learn to treat people, including ourselves, as whole beings – physically, emotionally, spiritually – we cannot then deal with another person as if with a machine for consuming. Nor do we want to tolerate a hospital treating us as lumps of flesh, or a school treating our children as vessels into which to pour knowledge and skills.'

Damian Randle in *Teaching Green* (Green Print).

emerging. The debate amongst green educators has been accordingly brisk: whether to simply take children on nature rambles or to launch them on a lifelong journey of spiritual discovery? Whether green ideas are best brought into the established system or whether they should become the foundation for a whole new system of education?

The answers to these questions will shape the day to day educational experiences of all our children – and they will determine the shape of the future.

LEARNING TO LIVE LIGHTLY

At the 'deep' end of green education is 'Earth Education'. Never mind mucking about with the odd nature walk or incorporating green ideas into the established curriculum, the Earth Educators aim straight for the soul.

If some of it has a rather far out, Californian ring, that's because the movement harks from the USA. But despite the language barrier, Earth Education seems to be taking off in Britain – as well as Canada, New Zealand and Australia.

'In the Institute for Earth Education we see ourselves as an educational arm of the deep ecology movement. We aim to develop and disseminate specific educational programmes that help people of all ages live more harmoniously and joyously with the natural world . . . The "supplementalists" are fond of saying that their goal is to teach students to think, not what to think. Our goal is to teach students why and how to live more lightly on the Earth and to help them develop a deeper personal relationship with it.'

Steve Van Matre, founder of the Institute for Earth Education and Professor of Environmental Education and Interpretation at Aurora University, Illinois, writing in *Green Teacher* magazine, no 12.

The Earth Education Institute has designed a series of courses – chiefly for teachers and group leaders – which enable them to take children on adventures. The idea is to create 'magical learning experiences' which focus on sharing and doing things at first hand. The old teaching methods of naming and labelling, showing and telling children are rejected. For instance, 'Sunship Earth' is a five-day programme which starts as a journey from a dimly lit room into deepest space. From here, the children can see planet Earth: very small, but rich in things to see, touch, smell, listen to and taste.

During the week, they will take part in a series of adventures, from invading a giant leaf disguised as a 'Chlorospy' to 'shrinking' to get an insect's eye view of the world. It's all about learning how this planet, the 'sunship', operates, and how they can both enjoy the ride and keep the ship going. And, in the process, the children have every opportunity to run about, get wet and dirty, or just sit quietly in the natural world.

In contrast, 'Earthwalks' are much shorter adventures (at about one hour) and are probably the most popular Earth Education programmes. The Earthwalk takes in about five or six activities, based on the five senses, all designed to show new ways of looking at familiar things in nature. Children sit quietly to listen to the sounds of nature before writing 'a song of the season'. They make a 'whiff cocktail' of pungent vegetation, and hold a mirror under their noses to make an 'eye in the sky' which gives a fresh view of the world.

'Earthkeepers' is a longer term adventure for ten to twelve year olds which takes place partly at school and partly at an outdoor centre. As with other Earth Education programmes, the idea is to help children understand basic ecological ideas and to develop enjoyment and understanding of the Earth and its life. It hinges around discovering the identity of the mysterious Earthkeeper 'E.M.' and earning your own set of 'keys' to the secret meanings of E.M. Say no more!

For details of Earth Education Workshops contact the British Earth Education Co-ordinator Ian Duckworth at Ufton Court Centre, Ufton Nervet, Berkshire RG7 4HD (tel: 0735 2920999), or Graham McDonald, Ballater Field Study Centre, Aberdeen AB3 5RJ (tel: 0339 55868).

Alternatively, for a wider range of activities – from family weekends to courses – contact Alan or Anna Dyer, Rainbow Cottage, Branscombe, near Seaton, Devon (tel: 029780 375). Their Earthworks organisation provides a whole range of outdoor learning experiences (based on Earth Education) to anyone who needs them – from WATCH groups to parents to the Countryside Commission. As a non-profitmaking organisation, they charge what people can afford.

Green Routes is a similar group which operates in the north of England and East Anglia. Sessions varying from half-day stints to week-long resource programmes are based on custom-designed Earth Education. They have a flexible approach catering for schools, activity holidays, voluntary youth groups, and leader training. Contact Martin Paine, Green Routes, 19 Castle Close, Castleton, North Yorkshire (tel: 0287 660108).

GREEN TEACHING

Bearded, sandalled, not exactly chic in his baggy tweed jacket, 'Superteach' is plodding along the corridor looking rather down in the mouth. Education, he muses, is being pushed inexorably towards narrow, anti-ecological, anti-human 'training for jobs'. Superteach is almost losing heart . . . Then – suddenly – *KAPOW* – *Green Teacher* magazine is here; Superteach metamorphoses into a caped crusader and he flies off to make sure that it gets into every staffroom in the country.

So runs the cartoon in *Green Teacher*, urging all those who work in education to subscribe. And GT is a fund of ideas, initiatives and news from the green educational front. It is run as a non-profitmaking co-operative with different co-editors for each issue.

Its 'general editor' is Damian Randle, who taught for twelve years before becoming joint-education officer at the Centre for Alternative Technology at Machynlleth in Wales. Randle has also written a book called *Teaching Green* (from Green Print, 1989) which is billed as a parents' guide to education for life on earth.

Although the book and the magazine are designed for teachers, teacher educators and curriculum developers, parents will also find them a treasure trove of stimulating and challenging ideas. *Green Teacher* costs £10 a year for six issues, from *Green Teacher*, Machynlleth, Powys, Wales SY20 8DN (tel: 0654 2141).

DRAMATIC CHANGE

'Two towns in the valley of Gaia were forever quarrelling and polluting each others' environments. One day the Spirits of the Lake decided they had had enough and set about teaching the people of the towns how to co-operate and take care of their valley.'

This is how *Resource* (the recycling magazine published by Avon Friends of the Earth) describes the plot of a play for schools. It is performed by Tsuba Theatre Company from Manchester as part of a series of performances, workshops and discussions aimed at raising the awareness of children about their environment. Contact Tsuba on 061 434 6448, and arrange for a performance for your school or children's group.

Drama is hard to beat as a way of fully engaging children's energies and attention. Hence the extraordinary success of the musical play written for children and teenagers called 'Peace Child' which has now clocked up over

600 productions involving over 10,000 children in almost a dozen countries. The Peace Child Foundation has been set up to cope with the demand, and the periodical *Peace Child's Progress* is reporting on the spread of this phenomenon around the world.

'Any school putting on 'Peace Child' can use all the children it can cram onto its stage for the crowd scenes, with others surging up and down the aisles singing 'I want to live!', expressing their horror of war and their conviction that peace is possible, natural and right beyond question.'
Terence Moore in *Green Teacher*, May 1989.

The basic story is one of American boy meets Soviet girl – and how, with their friends, they appeal to world leaders to stop the madness of the arms race. But no two productions are alike because the child actors take part in discussing the issues and modifying the script to reflect their own concerns. If you, your school or children's group are interested, contact Eirwen Harbottle, The London Centre for International Peacebuilding, Wickham House, 10 Cleveland Way, London E1 4TR.

The National Trust also runs the Young National Trust Theatre, a professional theatre-in-education company for older junior and secondary schoolchildren, which aims to get children thoroughly involved in the 'living history' which its dramas bring to life.

Sandpit Scholarship

'Most of what I really needed to know about how to live and what to do and how to be, I learned in Kindergarten. . . .

'Share everything. Play fair. Don't hit people. Put things back where you found them. Clean up your own mess. Don't take things that aren't yours. Say you're sorry when you hurt somebody. Wash your hands before you eat. Flush. Learn some and think some and play and work everyday some. When you go out into the world, watch for traffic, hold hands and stick together. Be aware of wonder. Remember the little seed in the plastic cup. The roots go down and the plant goes up and no one really knows how or why, but we are all like that. Goldfish and hamsters and white mice and even the little seed in the plastic cup – they all die.'

Robert Fulghum in *Green Teacher*, no 14.

BACK TO THE FUTURE

How does one week in your child's life affect the earth that we all live on? How much energy does he or she consume? How much waste does she or he produce – and what happens to it?

These are the questions which the 'Cabins Project' at the Centre for Alternative Technology in Wales was set up to tackle. A week in one of the Centre's specially-adapted cabins will give children the chance to learn the answers directly from their own experience. Each cabin is supplied with energy from renewable sources (solar or wind power, for example), and has its water supplied from a standpipe some distance away. All waste – human and vegetable – has to be disposed of in organically ecological ways.

> 'They will learn in the most practical ways possible about renewable energy supply and storage. If they want power for the radio, there are the aerogenerator, the photo-voltaics and the water turbines to be checked and the batteries and invertor to be monitored. If they want warm water, the solar collectors and/or woodstove must be dealt with. If the water supply is running low, new supplies must be fetched. They will see how the toilets contribute (in a no-smell way!) to the composting process, and each group will make at least a nominal contribution to food-growing work in the nearby organic plots.'
>
> From the 'Cabins Project' brochure, the Centre for Alternative Technology.

The centre now attracts some 60,000 visitors a year to see its displays of alternative energy generators, energy conservation measures and organic gardens. CAT also runs over fifty residential courses each year, many are for 'A' level and GCSE Technology, Science and Geography groups. A sampling of courses in recent years would include 'Alternative Technology activities for under 14s',

'Make It' (solar, wind and water projects for schools), and 'Craft, design, technology and Third World projects' with practical workshop sessions.

CAT also boasts a major exhibition on renewable energy, conservation and organic growing which is used as a resource for students' research. It holds a range of discussions, seminars and practical teaching sessions using the skills of its engineers, biologists and education staff. For more details get in touch with the Centre for Alternative Technology, Machynlleth, Powys, Wales SY20 9AZ (tel: 0654 2400). It is open daily except for Christmas Day and Boxing Day from 10 am to dusk (7 pm in the summer). Admission is £1.50 for concessions, £1.00 for children, and £6.50 for a family.

WORLD GAME

A new game for eleven to fourteen year olds, which tackles the thorny issues of environment and development in an entertaining way, has been devised jointly by people from Christian Aid and CAFOD, the Catholic Fund for Overseas Development. The game is called 'Breaking the Famine Cycle', and it works as a board game, with special 'development cards', dice and counters. Amongst the development cards, which can help a player win, are the 'Women's involvement', 'land security', 'peace' and 'sustainable agriculture' cards. The game is designed to lead children into discussions about how the cycle of famine and disaster can be broken – and about what we can do to help break it.

The game comes as part of a new pack from CAFOD/ Christian Aid called 'Handle With Care'. Contact London RE Teachers' Centre, Vauxhall Manor School, Lawn Lane, London SW8.

UNDER-FIVES

Britain has a lamentable record in pre-school education, with nurseries only available to a tiny minority of the neediest children. But a shining light in an otherwise gloomy prospect is provided by locally-based playgroups which are part of the Pre-school Playgroups Association. Based on the idea that children will learn through interesting, stimulating play – and through mixing with other pre-schoolers – playgroups depend on the close co-operation of parents within the community. (Unfortunately, fathers are much less involved than mothers.) Most of the work is voluntary although trained playgroup leaders do get paid a token sum.

Not only do children get tremendous enjoyment out of playgroups, but they meet the other local children who will probably go through the school system with them. Parents are also brought together to talk, work and watch their children interact. When so many modern families otherwise exist in small, isolated groupings, the benefits of a good playgroup are immeasurable.

If you want to find out about playgroups in your area or perhaps set up your own, contact the Pre-school Playgroups Association at 61–3 Kings Cross Road, London WC1X 9LL (tel: 071 833 0991).

SCHOOLS ON A HUMAN SCALE

There are several 'small schools' across the country which have survived the trend towards big 'high schools' on the American model. And in recent years a new generation of small schools has been springing up in accord with the 'small is beautiful' philosophy of the green movement.

One of the first of the new generation is actually called

> 'Small is beautiful applies as urgently to education as to economics. E.F. Schumacher wanted a society "as if people matter". We need schools "as if people matter". Such schools have to be of human scale.'
>
> From the Manifesto for Education on a Human Scale.

the Small School. It is a secondary school in Hartland, Devon. With the backing of the Schumacher Society, plus a great deal of support and involvement from parents, the Small School has become the working model for the campaign to run schools on 'Human Scale' principles.

Parents at Hartland were no longer prepared to bus their children some fifteen or twenty miles to a school with 1,800 pupils in a community where their children were not known. And so when Satish Kumar, President of the Schumacher Society, bought a converted chapel and two cottages on the main street of their village, a trust fund was established to buy these buildings for the new school. It kicked off in 1982 with nine children and one full-time teacher. The school can take a little over thirty pupils and it is now nearly full, with two full-time teachers and some sixteen visiting and part-time teachers, drawn from parents and people working in the neighbourhood. There are small fees for those who can afford it, and parents contribute materials, food or time – to type, teach, or to help with maintenance.

Food is local and vegetarian – for reasons of economy and hygiene – and children are closely involved in preparing and serving meals. They even bake their daily bread. There is a compulsory core curriculum and children do take GCSEs, although these are not allowed to dominate the curriculum. And children can choose their other subjects from a range which includes building, weaving, gardening, cheesemaking, sewing and knitting.

> 'Children who have come from other schools [to the Small School] have to reappraise teacher/pupil roles when the headteacher helps them with the washing-up.'
> Theresa West, who works at Hartland's Small School, in *Green Teacher*, no 6.

Parents, teachers and students from all over the world have approached the Small School, asking for places and looking for new ideas. But, by definition, one small school cannot take too many children. The Human Scale movement takes the view that when it is no longer possible for all the teachers to know all the children – and all the parents – then the school is too big.

But as the ill effects of size are being increasingly felt in modern education – with strained relations between teachers and children, bureaucracy, ill discipline, occasional truancy and even violence – the ideas of Human Scale education are gaining ground. And so much more is possible: in Denmark, small schools are flourishing with subsidies from the State which meet up to 80 per cent of costs.

For information and publications about the Human Scale movement and other small schools across the country, contact Human Scale Education Movement, c/o Dame Catherine's School, Ticknall, Derbyshire.

THE OTHERWISE OPTION

If you have ever had the awful experience of dragging your protesting child to school when she or he doesn't want to go, you may well have justified yourself by saying 'you have to go to school, it's compulsory'. Yet although school often feels compulsory, it isn't. We don't have to take our children to school. But we do have to provide them with education. The 1944 Education Act states that it is a parent's duty to make sure that children of school age 'receive efficient full-time education suitable to his [or her] age, aptitude and ability, either by regular attendance at school or otherwise'.

Thousands of parents in Britain take the 'otherwise' option by educating their children at home: some are unhappy with the ideas expressed in their child's school; some have children who are unhappy about going to school; some simply believe that school does have its merits, but that learning in the home environment is a richer and more rewarding preparation for the rest of life. Up to 15,000 are home-taught in Britain. After all, the institution of school as it is known in England is only little more than a century old.

'Schools have not been demonstrably successful in producing socially well-adjusted adults with a strong sense of community! There is no evidence that children who opt out of school fare any worse in this respect than those who stay in.'
Hazel and Alan Clawley in *Routes to Change*, published by the Green Party Education Working Group.

You don't have to be a teacher or to have any formal qualifications to educate your own children – although you are likely to be 'inspected' by the local authorities. Children can still take part in public exams, and it doesn't have to cost much. But you do have to enjoy the company of your children and be able and prepared to put aside other aspects of your life until they grow up.

There are two organisations who give information and support services for parents who are thinking of – or doing – home schooling. The biggest (with 2,000 members) is the self-help group Education Otherwise, 25 Common Lane, Hemingford Abotts, Cambridgeshire PE18 9AN (tel: 0480 63130). There is also the Children's Home-Based Education Association, 14 Basel Avenue, Armthorpe, Doncaster, Yorkshire.

Another useful consumer organisation for parents – and children – who want some basic advice or information about education is ACE, the Advisory Centre for Education. Their advisory service is there to help you with almost any aspect of education. Contact the Centre at 18 Victoria Park Square, London E2 9PB (tel: 081 980 4596).

COMMONWORK

Some of the most interesting ideas in green education are coming out of 'Commonwork' in Kent. This is an educational centre, farm and small brickworks near Sevenoaks, which welcomes groups of young people to take part in its wide range of projects.

Here are just some of Commonwork's ideas for projects to do with children – and, for the most part, there is no reason why parents and teachers shouldn't adapt them for their own use:

- Harvest celebrations: already, many schools are using the opportunity of this traditionally religious festival to broach some green ideas. (A harvest festival doesn't have to mean a formal religious ceremony.) Encourage children to collect blackberries from the hedgerows and to make jam; town children are always within reach of lanes and hedgerows. Make bread with them (most children love cooking) and have a go at some celebratory loaves for the festival.

- 'Ecology' means the study of homes: take children into woodland to build their own biodegradable shelters (but be careful not to institute your own forest clearances . . .). This will set them thinking about survival, about nature's raw materials – and about the difficulties of living in the wild. Or make shelters from non-biodegradable waste (plastic sacks from a farm, for instance). This provides food for thought on housing, on waste, on Third World shanty towns and the things we take for granted in our own homes. With younger children, try to make nests and model homes from straw and other materials. Or make nests and human homes out of clay.

- Take children to see milking in progress; many farm centres – or city farms – include this in their activities. At Commonwork, children take part in the milking and then go on to make their own yoghurt, discussing how the transformation takes place. They also take part in the feeding and care of calves. The aim is to give them some knowledge about the care (or lack of care) which we give domestic animals, and to learn some respect for the animal.

- Go in search of mini-beasts with nets for pond dipping, straws and matchboxes for 'pooting' (sucking tiny insects up through a straw and releasing them into a small box or jar). Sweep an area of trees or the margins of a park, common or field to find insects. But make sure you do the collection on site and release every creature back into its own environment.

- Give the children *carte blanche* to do a survey – at school, at home or on a local farm – into waste and recycling. At Commonwork, children are let loose to do their own investigative reporting, interviewing people working there, and are allowed to be genuinely critical when they think all is not as it should be. That's a rare opportunity, even in adult terms!

- Many of our day-to-day tasks are now mechanized – from driving to school to doing the laundry or vacuuming. Set children the challenge of achieving the same ends but by different means – whether that means walking, cycling, sweeping or handwashing. Talk about the different types of energy expended and how much effort is involved. (At Commonwork, children shift bales of straw and heaps of manure without benefit of tractors.) It all helps give a fresh view of machinery, energy and the meaning of modern life . . .

- Have a go at some interpretative artwork. Take the children out to look closely and sympathetically at some aspect of the outside world. Then set them to work with clay or paints. The Education Officer at Commonwork, Margaret Williams, says the children there have come up with some marvellous 'hedge pots' (pots with hedges all around) and 'grassland pots'. Even the smallest children will make shapes of leaves and trees they have seen. These are ideas that you can adapt to dough, playdough or plasticine.

- Commonwork have plenty of clay at their disposal: it lies just beneath the ground's surface. And they have made the most of it and the surrounding woods in their Stove Building Project, set up in conjunction with the development agency Intermediate Technology. Visiting young people can make simple cooking stoves – as used in the Third World – from the local clay. They can gather their own wood from the nearby woods.

The scope for learning is as wide as teachers want it to be – from simple identification of trees to the comparative fuel efficiency of open fires and stoves. Discussions can bring in the issue of saving trees around the world and the amount of time women spend in fetching wood and cooking.

For more information about Commonwork, contact the Education Co-Ordinator, Bore Place, Chiddingstone, near Edenbridge, Kent TN8 7AR (tel: 0732 463255).

DEVELOPMENT FOR PEOPLE

' "Development" and "environment" are different aspects of the same issue. Development throughout the world is only sustainable if it is ecologically sound. Many of today's environmental and development problems are a legacy of the western world's shortsighted exploitation of the earth's resources.'
From the Intermediate Technology booklet
What Can I Do.

The essentially green idea of one world (in which the earth and all its creatures are interdependent) is at the heart of the radical development charity Intermediate Technology. IT, as it's known, is based on the concepts of Schumacher, the well-known economist who wrote the classic green text *Small Is Beautiful*. IT is concerned with long-term development rather than emergency aid, and works with Third World people to make use of their own natural resources and surroundings. The aim is to help people to help themselves to make a living.

IT has its own youth organisation, run by young people, for young people, called Youth TAG (Technology Action Group) and it raises funds for IT's overseas projects and has its own quarterly magazine.

> Reporter: 'Mr Gandhi, what do you think of Western civilization?'
> Mr Gandhi: 'I think it would be a good idea.'

IT also has an active Education Department which is bringing some very challenging ideas – on development, on women's work, on racism, to name but a few – into the classroom. Their educational resources include slides, videos, books and a range of publications. Some of their projects (in Design and Technology for instance) are structured to fit into the National Curriculum.

For further information on IT or a copy of their resource list, contact The Education Department, Intermediate Technology, Myson House, Railway Terrace, Rugby, Warwickshire CV21 3HT.

For school leavers, two of the IT leaflets could be especially helpful: *What Can I Do* lists courses in develop-

One Day in the Life of an African Woman

I T suggests the following simple – but revealing – project. They describe a day in the life of a woman in the Third World, who may work some sixteen hours a day even when pregnant, and may go back to work within a few days of delivery:

04.45 Wakes up, washes, eats some left-over food
05.00 Walks to the fields, leaving grand-mother or older children to look after infants
05.30 Ploughs, hoes, weeds and plants
15.00 Collects firewood and comes home
16.00 Pounds and grinds grain
17.30 Fetches water 2 kilometres each way, using a pot weighing some 20 kilos
18.30 Lights fire, cooks family meal
19.30 serves food to family and eats
20.30 Washes the children, the dishes and herself
21.30 Goes to bed.

Now, suggests IT, children could keep a daily diary for their mother or the person who looks after them, then make a twenty-four hour pie chart for each woman's day – and compare the two.

ment studies as well as other action to take in furthering sustainable development; *Voluntary Work for the School Leaver in Countries Overseas* gives details of work opportunities in the Third World.

PARENTS TAKING PART

- What takes place at school is only a part of the learning process. Draw on the ideas in this book to talk to your children about environmental issues, and ask what they think about it all. Who knows, *you* might learn something? (If you do want to extend your own knowledge, many Local Education Authorities run evening classes on environmental issues, as does the Workers Educational Association.)

- If you have already established a system of recycling at home, why not suggest that the school does the same? Many schools are already raising sums of money for charities by recycling cans, and enthusiastic children are keen to get their hands on anything that responds to a magnet (such as aluminium).

- Get to know the teachers at your local school. You'll soon find out who is supportive of green ideas. Be prepared to help with project work or to provide information on environmental issues.

- Keep an eye out for interesting events, films, television programmes, books and games with a green theme – and put them your children's way.

GREENING YOUR SCHOOL OR COLLEGE

Picture this: dedicated green teacher describing the tragedy of the rainforests and the need for energy conservation – while pupils in their short sleeves gasp for air near windows thrown open to let the heat out. It happens in schools, colleges, libraries and other institutions across the country. There's little point in teaching children the theories of environmental problems while their own educational establishment is a lesson in how to waste energy unnecessarily.

Why not encourage pupils to set up their own 'energy audit' at school or college? Earth Action (the Friends of the Earth Youth Group) has drawn up the following system as a guide to giving your establishment a mark out of one hundred for its energy use:

- Check doors, windows and their frames from draughts. (Score out of 15)
- Check to see if walls and roofs are insulated throughout the establishment. (Score out of 30)
- Check to see how high a proportion of windows are south facing. (Score out of 5)
- Check to see if windows are double glazed. (Score out of 10)
- Check to see if floors are insulated and carpets underlayed. (Score out of 15)
- Check that none of the rooms are too hot. (Score out of 10)
- Check to see how careful people are with the way they conserve energy, teachers included. (Score out of 10)

With the help of a sympathetic teacher, take the findings and suggestions (about insulation, double glazing and so on) to the head or bursar. Point out that although most energy-saving programmes mean investment, in the long run they save money. And, of course, they have great environmental benefits. Head teachers are looking for ways to save money – so this is a good opportunity to argue for more careful use of energy at school.

Many teachers wouldn't care less, nor have schools the money for window repairs etc.

YOUNG VEGETARIANS

The youth wing of the Vegetarian Society also has two well organized campaigns for school children. Together with Animal Aid and the Athene Trust they launched the 'Choice!' campaign for the right to choose a healthy vegetarian meal at school. Nine thousand secondary school children were asked what they thought of the 'vegetarian' meals provided at school, and 70 per cent said these were either 'bad' or 'appalling'. The Choice! campaign provides a pack for school caterers, a pack for school children, and gives tips to children on the best way to tackle the issue at school.

SCREAM!! is the School Campaign for Reaction Against Meat, which provides children with some pretty strong ammunition about cruelty to animals. It also encourages them to collect signatures for the Choice! petition (aimed at local education authorities) and to write to the Minister of Agriculture to protest about the conditions of animals kept in factory farms and slaughterhouses.

> 'Can you imagine being locked in a classroom in semi-darkness, unable to move from your desk, turn around or even go to the toilet – for months on end!
>
> 'Now you've an idea what factory farms are like.'
>
> SCREAM!! campaign poster,
> The Vegetarian Society.

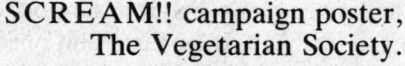

For more information on young vegetarian activities, contact Juliet Gellatley at the Vegetarian Society, Park-

dale, Dunham Road, Altrincham, Cheshire WA14 4QG
(tel: 061 928 0793); and see Food.

IDEAS IN GREEN TEACHING

- 'The World in a Supermarket Bag: An Activity on
  Food for 7–11 Year Olds' is a project to stimulate
  children's interest in the way our food links us to the
  rest of the world. Find out more from the Youth and
  Education Department, Oxfam, 274 Banbury Road,
  Oxford OX2 7DZ (tel: 0865 56777).
- *Points of View – Nature Conservation Leaflets for
  Schools*: this is a series of leaflets for teachers and
  students designed to introduce the current controver-
  sial issues concerning the British countryside – it
  covers hedgerows, boating, and nitrates. It is free if
  you send an A4 stamped addressed envelope to the
  Nature Conservancy Council, Environmental Education Section, Northminster House, Peterborough PE1
  1UA (tel: 0733 40345).
- 'Human Numbers, Human Needs': how can we maintain the balance between the size of the human race,
  its needs and the Earth's resources? This slide-pack,
  with teacher's notes, tackles the issue. It costs £15 (or
  £25 for the video version) from International Planned
  Parenthood Federation Distribution Unit, Regent's
  College, Inner Circle, Regent's Park, London NW1
  4NS.
- *Naturally Special: Field Studies with People that have
  Special Needs*: this paper is an account of how special
  needs students can participate in day and residential
  programmes which bring them into closer contact with
  the natural environment, it costs £4 from Mike Clat-
  worthy, National Association of Field Studies Offi-

cers, Stansfield Field Study Centre, Quarry Road, Headington Quarry, Oxford OX3 8SB.

- The National Association for Environmental Education has a series of practical guides including: *Traffic Study and Survey; An Incubator in the Classroom; Creating and Maintaining a Garden to attract Butterflies;* and *Developing a School Nature Reserve.* Send a stamped addressed envelope for a full list of publications to N A E E, West Midlands College of Higher Education, Gorway, Walsall, West Midlands WS1 3BD (tel: 0922 31200).

- *Ecological and Environmental Education Initiatives in Britain* is a list of ecology and conservation projects which are funded by local or central government schemes or initiated by local groups. It aims to provide a source of up-to-date information on current projects. It costs £6 from Urban Spaces Scheme, Polytechnic of North London, Holloway Road, London N7 8DB.

- 'Project Ecology' is a series of information and activity books from the publishers Wayland. It includes *Urban Ecology*, *Air Ecology*, *Animal Ecology*, *Land Ecology*, *Plant Ecology* and *Water Ecology*. The books are £6, from booksellers.

- The Centre for Environmental Education produces a newsheet detailing materials, resources and events in environmental education. Contact C E E, School of Education, University of Reading, London Road, Reading RG1 5AQ. Ten issues cost £4.50 a year, or they are free from Local Education Authorities subscribing to C E E.

- For a full price list of books, pamphlets, study kits, teaching and display packs, posters and audio-visual programmes on green issues, contact The Conservation Trust, National Centre for Environmental Education, George Palmer Site, Northumberland Avenue, Reading, Berks RG2 7PW (tel: 0734 868442). And turn to Pollution for more projects.

- The National Trust have an Education Manager to expand their education policy and work closely with education authorities. The Trust is very keen to encourage children to visit its sites in the company of teachers or parents. Teachers' packs and schoolrooms are provided at some properties. For more information contact 36 Queen Anne's Gate, London SW1 (tel: 071 222 9251).

5

Pollution

*the big issues * taking action*
* *Young Friends of the Earth*
* *toxic waste hazards * dioxins * air * water*
* *saving water * seas and beaches * cancers*
* *pregnancy * nuclear hazards **

'The human race has been very successful at
contaminating almost every part of our
planet, from the upper atmosphere to the
depths of the oceans.'
                    Earth Action (Friends of the Earth
                        Youth Section) pollution leaflet.

CONTAMINATION BEYOND OUR CONTROL?

Pollution is a pretty large topic these days. Excellent
books have been written about most aspects of it, and
major environmental organisations like Friends of the
Earth and Greenpeace are campaigning to prevent it

worldwide. But in what respect does pollution affect parents and children?

The destruction of the rainforests, acid rain, the greenhouse effect, global warming, ozone depletion: all of these urgent and potentially catastrophic issues are linked to pollution. They are a threat to our children's future. But they can seem very remote, as if nothing we can do will have an impact.

In fact, the reverse is true. The day-to-day choices we all make about how to live on this earth add up to the sum of the problems. By taking responsibility for our own part in pollution, we can be part of the solution. And by being aware of the issues, by being alert to how pollution affects the air our children breathe, the water they drink, the earth they walk on, we have a better chance of safeguarding their health.

THE BIG ISSUES

- **Acid rain:** we are sending a cocktail of pollutants into the atmosphere causing acidification of soil and water – and resulting in damage to all creatures who depend on these for their survival. Britain's trees are amongst the most damaged in Europe. Sulphur emissions from our power-stations must be cleaned up.
- **Rainforests:** fifty million acres of Brazil's irreplaceable forests are disappearing in the space of each year. One species becomes extinct every half-hour as a result. Rainforest destruction could change the world's climate with devastating effects.
- **Greenhouse effect:** many of our daily activities (the use of electricity from power-stations, driving cars, consuming the products of industry and agriculture) contribute to changes which warm up the atmosphere

and oceans. Sea level rises in the next century could result, while many fertile lands could become unproductive.

- **The ozone layer:** CFCs (chlorofluorocarbons) are gases used in a wide variety of processes. But when they reach the upper atmosphere they break down the ozone layer – which absorbs up to 99 per cent of the sun's damaging ultraviolet rays. Skin cancer, and damage to plants and marine life, may well be the result.

- **Water pollution:** many of our rivers are now little more than open sewers, contaminated by pesticides and fertilizers, farmyard waste and industrial effluent. The North Sea and the Irish Sea are filthy with chemicals and sewage.

- **Radiation and nuclear power:** nuclear accidents at Three Mile Island, Windscale and Chernobyl have shown how the invisible menace of radiation can devastate whole communities – even across continental boundaries. The Irish Sea is now the most radioactively contaminated sea in the world.

What you can do:

- Conserve energy: try to insulate your home as much as possible to prevent heat loss. Turn off all electrical appliances when not in use and invest in some low energy light bulbs (see Home). Avoid buying non-essential electrical appliances: try sharing or renting machinery which you don't use very often.

- Insulate yourself and your children with warm clothes: this is a most efficient way to save fuel.

- Find out if your council runs an energy advice centre. Some councils will help you save on fuel bills with a 'domestic energy audit'.

- Be less of a consumer: practically everything you buy

bears an energy cost in terms of energy used to make it, transport and packaging.

- Together with your children keep your eyes open for examples of environmental pollution. If you spot a smokey chimney, foam or dead fish in a river or stream, phone the council's Environmental Health Officer.

- If you see someone dropping litter, pick it up and give it back to them. If you see someone emptying rubbish from their car, take their number and report it to the police.

- Reuse and recycle bottles, cans and newspapers (see Home).

- Reject the pressures to clean your home like a white tornado. All those detergents and bleaches end up polluting our rivers and killing wildlife. Use environmentally-friendly products.

- Don't pour poison down the drain: weedkillers, paint and medicines should be disposed of safely. Ask your local council about civic amenity sites with special disposal points.

- Use your car less, public transport more. Apart from the energy and materials used in making cars, motor vehicles generate more air pollution than any other human activity.

- Talk about the problems of pollution with your friends and your children. Offer to help teachers prepare classroom materials on pollution and the tropical rain forests.

- Don't buy tropical hardwood furniture, joinery or timber unless it is sustainably produced (in Britain, only 5 per cent of tropical hardwood imports are). Friends of the Earth has a Tropical Hardwoods Product List which will put you in the picture.

- Avoid buying CFC areosols, foam packaging and

foamed insulation materials. CFCs must be banned immediately.

STAND UP AND BE COUNTED

On the wider political level too, we must press for some important changes. We must stop the destruction of the rainforests and start replanting. The international timber trade, and aid agencies like the World Bank, must change their policies to make conservation a priority. Friends of the Earth have been negotiating with the Timber Trade Federation to regulate the industry and to make sure that our tropical hardwood imports come from sustainable sources. Action by conservationists, including FoE, has already caused the World Bank to review its road building programme in north-west Amazonia, and has prompted the American and British governments to reconsider some trade and aid policies which are hastening the destruction of rain forests.

On the domestic energy front, nuclear power must be phased out as soon as possible. We must burn less coal and oil, and develop the renewable energy sources (wind, waves and solar power).

These changes can no longer wait. Ask your local councillors and MPs what their policies are, and join local and national environmental groups. Friends of the Earth and Greenpeace have been working hard to combat pollution. Friends of the Earth can be contacted at 26–8 Underwood Street, London N1 7JQ (tel: 071 490 1555); Greenpeace at 30–1 Islington Green, London N1 8XE (tel: 071 354 5100).

EARTH ACTION

When it comes to combating pollution, many young people have a lot to teach their parents. In terms of taking direct, effective and well-organized action, Earth Action – the youth section of Friends of the Earth – has been taking the lead. Set up in 1988, within a year and a half there were over seventy groups in action and many more getting off the ground. The idea is to provide a focus for young people (aged fourteen to twenty-three) to get involved in campaigning on environmental issues by joining – or starting – local groups of their own.

> 'This will be the last generation that can have any impact on saving the rain forests. When [they] are gone we will have lost over half the world's wild species. Deforestation will disrupt global weather patterns which will cause more severe droughts and floods like those already occurring in Africa and Asia.'
>
> Earth Action Organiser

To start an Earth Action group, it's a good idea for young people to get together with friends who have similar ideas. The next step is to contact the Earth Action office at Friends of the Earth. They will help a group get started by supplying leaflets, giving advice on producing posters and suggesting other young people in the area who may be interested.

Activities are based around a series of 'Days of Action' – publicizing and raising awareness on issues like global warming, acid rain and the rain forests. Members have leafleted the public, lobbied companies with fleets of cars on cutting vehicle emissions, and have taken direct action on the use of whale fat in beauty products by standing outside shops and naming the products to shoppers. There is action on local problems, too, like setting up recycling schemes.

New members will get the Earth Action Pack with practical information about how to get organized. The Earth Action Report (EAR), a bi-monthly newsletter, follows, keeping groups up-to-date with each other and with planned events and Days of Action.

Earth Action claim their Day of Action (January 28th, 1989) on global warming was a huge success, with groups all over the country going out onto the streets dressed in wetsuits to highlight the effects of rising sea levels. A group from Harlow College placed a canoe in the town centre to make their point, while Wye College Earth Action stood in a rubber dinghy, and Farnham Earth Action built a greenhouse in the local high street. They were amongst the 150 Friends of the Earth and Earth Action groups who took action to warn people about the risks associated with the greenhouse effect. They got plenty of press coverage – local and national – in their concerted attempt to raise public awareness.

And what about younger children? According to Julie Brown, Earth Action co-ordinator at FoE, children under fourteen may well be included in future initiatives. Meanwhile, one FoE group in Muswell Hill, London, has already set up its own junior section.

HAZARDS OF WASTE

Once upon a time there was a big chemical company, called Hooker, near the Niagara Falls, USA. In the 1940s it began to dump chemical wastes in an abandoned canal connected to the Niagara River. Later, this was earthed over and an elementary school was built on the site.

When many people fell ill, locals got suspicious. Eventually the area had to be evacuated and the school was pulled down. Today, the name Love Canal stands for what can happen when industry puts its profits before people – and the environment. (Hooker continued to pollute – on different sites – despite legal action by the US Environmental Protection Agency.)

Do we have any Love Canals in Britain? According to Peter Bunyard and Fern Morgan-Grenville in *The Green Alternative* we simply don't know – because no one has looked. No accurate record has been kept of abandoned dumps in this country: there is no chart to the minefield. Yet in 1985 an independent consultancy firm estimated that there could be a hazard from some 600 landfills across the country.

And the problems look set to worsen in the future. 'Europe's toxic waste timebomb ticks away'; 'Lack of controls on toxic waste is "building disaster" '; 'Growth of toxic waste disposal trade becomes burning issue': headlines like these crop up again and again.

No one knows for sure how much hazardous waste is produced in Britain, but one CBI (Confederation of British Industry) estimate sets the figure at 12 million tonnes a year. The implications for all of us are alarming, but – as ever – small children and pregnant women are amongst the most vulnerable. This is why, in 1989, outside the Rechem plant near Pontypool, a group of young mothers protested with their children that the toxic chemicals incinerator was unsafe. As members of MACAR (Mothers and Children Against Rechem), they said they were worried about the future health of their children in an environment which they believe to be polluted by toxic fumes. Local people had been complaining about sore eyes, tight chests and feelings of sickness. Levels of poisonous PCBs (polychlorobiphenyls) had been found in duck eggs which were sixty times greater than in a sample of eggs which was clear of contamination.

BEWARE DIOXIN

'Dioxin is generally agreed to be the most dangerous chemical known. Disagreement amongst the scientific community stems from what level can be assumed safe for humans.'

Women's Environmental Network in
Dioxin, A Briefing.

Dioxin is an artificially produced, extremely toxic by-product of various chemical reactions. It comes from the chlorine-bleaching processes of the paper industry, municipal and industrial waste incinerators, some pesticides and herbicides, and car exhaust fumes. Once in the environment, dioxins tend to build up through the food chain – until they contaminate women's breastmilk. A World Health Organisation study in 1988 showed that dioxin has reached the top of the food chain and that today's children are getting much higher doses than their parents ever did.

There is no dispute about the havoc which dioxin causes to wildlife and the environment. As for people, the ill-effects range from headaches and nausea to liver and kidney damage and neuro-psychiatric symptoms. In the long term it is thought to affect the reproductive and immune systems, causing birth defects (like spina bifida) and possibly cancer.

'Women deposit fat stores along with dioxins in their body during pregnancy. Slimming and stress release fat deposits and therefore toxic chemicals into the body giving much higher doses.'

Women's Environmental Network in
Dioxin, *A Briefing*.

What you can do:

- Avoid chlorine-bleached paper products, especially sanitary products.
- Use re-cycled paper products.
- Avoid food – like milk – which is packaged in paper cartons. Dioxins may migrate from paper into food.
- Contact the Women's Environmental Network who are campaigning around this issue at 287 City Road, London EC1V 1LA (tel: 071 490 2511).

'Britain and the rest of the EEC is facing a toxic waste crisis because industry produces 50 per cent more waste than can be disposed of at existing facilities.

'As a result, thousands of tons of toxic waste is exported, often to be dumped in Third World countries or dealt with in the Eastern bloc.'

Paul Brown in the *Guardian*, 16 May 1989.

AIR

Fresh air. Our birthright. Many of us were brought up with the idea that children should run around in it as much as possible. And that since the days of the notorious pea-soupers (the London smog of 1952 killed 4,000 people), our air is much cleaner.

Although our city air does look much cleaner these days, toxic vehicle fumes are putting the health of ten million Britons at risk. Friends of the Earth say that air pollution may have caused up to a fifth of lung cancers. Amongst the most vulnerable groups – as usual – are small children and pregnant women.

'Some of the chemicals in typical urban smog have been found to alter DNA in cells, causing cancer and birth defects. More subtly, it also suppresses the immune system by reducing lymphocity and antibody production, making us more susceptible to illness.'
Karen Christensen in *Home Ecology* (Arlington Books).

And of course, the environment is a victim too, as pollution from factories and cars make rain water acid, causing the 'acid rain' which is slowly destroying Europe's lakes and forests. Acid rain also washes essential nutrients from soils and raises the level of toxic metals in water.

One of the pollutants to emerge from car exhaust fumes is ozone – and while we need it to stay intact in the ozone layer above our heads, down on the ground it damages crops and trees, and contributes to global warming.

Ozone is a 'secondary' pollutant formed by a photochemical reaction when sunlight reacts with nitrogen oxides and hydrocarbons. The highest levels occur when spells of hot weather combine with heavy traffic producing 'photochemical smog'.

WATCH (the junior wing of the Royal Society for Nature Conservation) has launched The Ozone Project for schoolchildren. The idea is for children to monitor low-level ozone by growing and observing the ozone sensitive nicotiana plant. The greater the levels of ozone (which can cause coughing, headaches, and damage to lungs and plants) the more spots will appear on the plants' leaves. The results will be collated to provide a map of low-level ozone pollution in Britain – which can then be compared to the Department of the Environment's own results. The Ozone Project Pack is £5 from the Ozone Project, Freepost (SL1647), Slough SL2 3BH.

'One in five people in Britain is at risk from smog, mainly caused by vehicle exhaust fumes. Our research shows that infants under two years, pregnant women and the elderly are the most vulnerable. Health problems such as asthmas, bronchitis and heart conditions are aggravated. We urge people to protect their health by avoiding strenuous exercise until pollution levels have lowered.' Smog alert, July 1989, from Friends of the Earth to the media.

The World Health Organisation published guidelines on pollution levels in 1987, but Britain is regularly over the recommended limits. WHO guidelines for ozone were exceeded several times during the hot summer of 1989 which saw some of the highest levels since 1976. Both rural and urban areas were affected; one Devon site reached 135 parts per billion (the WHO upper limit is 100 ppb).

Carbon monoxide levels also exceeded the WHO guideline of 10mg/m3 over an eight-hour period for twenty-four days during the autumn of 1988 at one London site. The highest reading was almost double the WHO guideline.

Photochemical smog causes:
- irritation of the eyes, nose and throat;
- and it is linked to respiratory ailments like asthma.

Long-term effects include:
- reduced resistance to infection
- headaches
- bronchitis
- conjunctivitis
- chronic depression
- nausea
- skin rashes
- lead poisoning
- lung cancer.

Countries like Japan, Switzerland, the Netherlands and the USA have mandatory air quality standards. Pollution alerts are broadcast by the media when levels are high, warning people to stay indoors and not to go out jogging. Some governments have the power to curb car use and to make factories shut down until the air improves. But in

Britain, it was Friends of the Earth who issued smog alerts to the press as ozone levels soared in the heat of 1989. Since then the government has announced plans to inform the public whenever ozone levels get too high, but there are no plans for warnings about other toxic fumes – or for introducing air quality standards comparable to those in other countries.

British power-stations are still producing the pollutant sulphur dioxide, although investment in pollution control equipment could cut this down. Power-stations also contribute a third of nitrogen dioxide pollution which causes acid rain and problems to the lungs.

But a major air pollution culprit is the car. It produces nearly a half of nitrogen dioxide pollution, as well as 85 per cent of carbon monoxide pollution, plus ozone. Yet traffic is set to double over the next thirty-five years.

WHAT CAN YOU DO?

- If you live in the 'Big Smoke', try to take small children along the quieter roads with less chance of lorries belching exhaust fumes over the buggy. And take them to run about in what's left of our wide open spaces whenever you can.
- Keep children and cigarette smoke as far apart as possible, and if you are pregnant or hoping to be, try not to smoke.
- Cut down on your car use and make sure it is running as cleanly and efficiently as possible (see Transport).
- Don't buy aerosols.
- Conserve energy (see Home).
- Plant a tree. National Tree Week is arranged annually by the Woodland Trust, with activities from coppice planting to rhododendron clearing. Their aim is to

keep Britain's threatened landscape as leafy as possible. Contact the Woodland Trust at Autumn Park, Dysart Road, Grantham, Lincolnshire NG31 6LL.

- Support the Friends of the Earth Clean Air campaign. They produce excellent briefing documents and recommend how to go about making official complaints about air pollution – and how to make your voice heard. FoE have three main aims: the public should be informed when pollution levels are high; local authorities should have powers to close factories and control vehicle use; and the British government should introduce air quality standards in line with WHO guidelines.

- Send off for the Air Pollution Pack. This is a school's pack from the National Council for Clean Air which contains a set of illustrated fact sheets suitable for nine to eleven year olds, plus activity and experiment sheets for teachers. Pollution problems – including smog, lead, acid rain, asbestos and the greenhouse effect – are explained. The pack also describes experiments you can do with standard classroom equipment, and suggests other classroom activities and fieldwork studies. It might also be fun at home! It costs £1 from NCCA, 136 North Street, Brighton BN1 1RG (tel: 0273 26313).

- Write to your MP or MEP asking for their support for clean air.

WATER

In Britain, a generation of parents has grown up with the idea that water is 'safe' and water is 'free'. You turn on the tap and there it is: as much as you like – to drink, wash with or squander – at no extra cost.

We are rapidly being disillusioned. Consumers are

becoming increasingly aware of how many potentially dangerous pollutants we take in with every tumblerful of water.

According to a report in the *Guardian* (14 September, 1989), the threat to our water supply is the worst since the times of the Victorian cholera epidemics. Each of the country's 400 principal water treatment plants face an average of six major pollution threats a year. Lesser – but still serious – incidents have been occurring at the rate of six a day. In 1984, thousands of people were affected by a liquid phenol spill into the River Dee. In 1989, the drinking water supply of several million people in the Banbury area was affected when a sewage spill passed through a treatment works undetected. And in 1988, 7,000 people in Cornwall drank water polluted with two tonnes of liquid aluminium sulphate. The long-term effects of such an aluminium dose are unknown.

'Chemicals such as tranquillisers and contraceptive hormones which have passed through the human body have also been detected in "cleaned" water. Little is known about the effects of the 1,200 or so other micropollutants which have been discovered in drinking water . . . In 1981 the Water Research Council reported that "most" of the 343 organic compounds it had identified in drinking water "have never been evaluated in terms of safety".'

From *The Green Alternative* by Peter Bunyard and Fern Morgan-Grenville (Methuen).

Privatisation of water seems unlikely to improve matters. The new private water companies have to give details of their water quality in their annual reports – but these will refer to how the water was eighteen months previously. And, as yet, there is no provision for warnings to households with children or pregnant women (or ill or old people) should water standards be breached.

> 'Babies and young children are particularly at risk from nitrate, pesticide and heavy metal pollution. Even if we act now, the problems will probably worsen for at least twenty years.'
>
> John Button in *How To Be Green* (Century Hutchinson).

Lead

A particular worry is lead in water. Lead damages children's brains – as well as causing nerve damage and anaemia. Houses all over the country still have lead pipes installed before 1976 when lead was banned from use in water pipes.

What can you do? Ask your local water authority (in the phone book under 'water') to check the lead content of the water that comes out of your taps. They should do this free of charge and some will give grants to replace lead pipes. Meanwhile, run your taps for a few minutes before drinking the water: this flushes the pipes out and reduces lead concentration. But it is also a waste of water, so get your pipes checked as soon as possible.

Nitrates

Nitrate levels in British drinking water have risen alarmingly in recent years, as nitrogen fertilizers used by farmers are washed into the water supply. About four million people – mostly in the south-east of the country – are getting water which has higher nitrate levels than the EEC 'Maximum Admissible Concentration'.

> 'High levels of nitrates can also increase the risk of a very rare blood disease, methaemoglobinaemia (where the blood's ability to carry oxygen is diminished). This occurs in bottlefed babies whose feeds are made up with tap water. In Hull last year [1988], the level of nitrates was so high that babies were supplied with bottled water on the National Health Service.'
>
> *Radio Times*, 3–9 June, 1989.

This brings the risk of 'blue-baby syndrome', in which a small baby's ability to absorb oxygen is reduced. Although the full syndrome is rare, there are worries that newborns may suffer lesser degrees of oxygen deficiency which may go unnoticed. (It's also another reason for breastfeeding; nitrates do not seem to pass into the breast-milk to any significant extent.) According to Friends of the Earth, older children and pregnant women may also suffer adverse health effects. There is thought to be a link between high nitrate levels and stomach cancer.

What can you do about nitrates?

There is no ideal way to avoid nitrates. But there are various measures you can take to cut down the levels in your family's drinks – and in foods.

Water filters are sold to purify tap water, but they don't do much to reduce nitrate levels. However you can buy separate nitrate-removing cartridges for filters, which should be more effective. Boiling the water doesn't help: in fact it may concentrate the nitrates, increasing the risk.

> 'Some European mineral water was recently measured with radiation levels seventeen times the World Health Organisation's recommended limits, and high levels of bacterial contamination are by no means uncommon. Because mineral water is not chlorinated, bacteria levels can rise steeply if it is stored in shops or in the larder for some time before being drunk. The Consumer's Association found a high incidence of bacterial contamination of mineral water, in tests conducted in early 1989.'
> From *Nitrates: The Threat to Food and Water*
> by Nigel Dudley (Green Print).

You could buy bottled water. But this is a highly expensive and energy wasteful option (according to John Button, bottled water costs 1,000 times as much as tap water in terms of energy). And bottled water may be polluted with other substances – as in the benzene scare that caused Perrier to withdraw 160 million bottles in February 1990.

Also in February 1990, the *Observer* reported that the majority of bottled water fail to meet minimum standards laid down for domestic drinking water, according to American research. Among the substances found that were above limits for Europe, the USA and the WHO, were aluminium (linked to premature senile dementia) and the highly-poisonous metal, mercury.

One way to counteract some of the possible side-effects of nitrates is to eat plenty of fresh, organically-grown vegetables – which are believed to protect against nitrates. But also, take care to avoid the kinds of vegetables which are themselves likely to build up high nitrate levels – such as spinach, lettuce, celery, fennel, beetroot, turnip, radish and cornsalad. Any nitrate-storing vegetables will build up high nitrate levels when grown under glass – whether they are organic or not. So avoid eating these vegetables out of season. Nitrates in meat can be avoided by buying organically-grown, additive-free meat. Or by going vegetarian.

Nitrate Action

- If you are bottlefeeding your baby and nitrate levels in your area are known to be high, ask your health visitor or local health authority (look in the phone book) if you are eligible for bottled water to reduce the baby's nitrate intake.
- Join one of the campaigning organisations (like Friends of the Earth) who are working against nitrate pollution.
- Write to your water authority (in the phone book under 'water') and ask about levels of nitrate in your tap water.
- Contact your local paper about the levels of nitrate in your area and ask them to write about it.

- Suggest to your local school or college that they run a project and mount an exhibition about local nitrate levels.
- Write to your MP or MEP about your feelings.

Pesticides

Pesticides can be poisonous to humans – as well as the weeds, insects and plant diseases which they are designed to kill off. Unfortunately, these chemicals are being washed into our water supply to such an extent that the British Geological Survey in 1987 warned of 'a pesticide pollution timebomb'. At least sixteen toxic pesticides are commonly found in drinking water.

The experts are still maintaining that the traces of pesticides found in drinking water are so low that we have no need to worry. (Haven't we heard that before . . . ?) Yet Friends of the Earth say the effects of small quantities of pesticides being ingested by the body over many years are unknown.

Apart from joining the bottled-water bandwagon (see page 146), the most effective thing you can do is campaign for change.

Aluminium

There is evidence of a possible link between the aluminium levels of water and Alzheimer's disease (or senile dementia). However, the water companies are unconvinced, and some continue to add aluminium to drinking water to make it clearer. In some areas, aluminium enters drinking water after acid rain has washed it from the soil. A good water filter will reduce aluminium.

TESTING THE WATER

Your local authority is legally bound to provide data on water quality, and even the government admits that at least two million people are using tap water that exceeds health limits for nitrates and aluminium. Friends of the Earth have a Water Campaign, contact their central office, 26–8 Underwood Street, London N1JQ (tel: 071 490 1555), which produces a very useful and informative briefing sheet called *Drinking water: is it up to standard*. This explains how to find out about the quality of your tap water and where to direct any complaints. It includes a form produced by the European Commission for making complaints about failure to comply with EEC law.

Or, if you simply want your own quick and simple test to monitor water, the 'Aquatest' (now available from chemists and healthfood shops at about £3.99) will give you the answers within a quarter of an hour. With its easy-to-read colour chart, it should be fun for the children too.

WATER DOWN THE DRAIN

Only recently are we becoming more aware of just what our drinking water supply really 'costs'. In terms of the environment, there is the loss of farmland and valleys, flooded to make reservoirs, and the Scottish forests cut down for the same reason. There is the industrial effluent and domestic pollution that we flush through the system and into our rivers and seas with devastating effects for all forms of life – including our own. There is the expensive treatment process with all its use of 'purifying' chemicals. And the fact that we are using up the underground water supplies: all over the world, these aquifers are shrinking through over-consumption of their water.

Down the Spout

All the water that comes through our taps is supposed to be of drinking water quality, yet most goes straight down the drain:

- 33 per cent is flushed down the toilet
- 17 per cent is used for washing ourselves
- 12 per cent goes through the washing machine or dishwasher
- only 0·008 per cent is actually drunk.

STEPS TO SAVE WATER

- Give the children a shower rather than a bath. The water for one bath is worth fifteen minutes in the shower – and you'll save energy on hot water too.
- Only use washing machines – or dishwashers – when they are full.
- For outside use – from plant watering to car washing – install a good old-fashioned water butt under a roof gutter.
- If you run the tap while teeth are being cleaned, five litres of water are likely to go down the drain. Try using a tooth mug instead.
- Mend all leaks. A dripping tap wastes some thirty litres of water a day.

As our children grow up, it is likely that water will be metred. That may well put an end to many a paddling pool, and families on low incomes will have to choose between hygiene and the expense of water. But whether or not metering is a fair solution, something has to be done to curb our waste of water.

POLLUTED SEAS, POLLUTED BEACHES

The Great British Beach is an essential part of our mythology of childhood. Every summer, come rain (usually) or shine, there was no healthier way for a child to pass the holidays than down on the sand with the bucket and spade brigade.

Alas, the modern British child may catch gastroenteritis – or some far more serious health hazards – with his or her bucket full of crabs. Each year, the sea around Britain is used as a dumping ground for:

- nine million tons of sewage sludge
- forty-two million tons of dredged spoil (such as harbour silt)
- over two million tonnes of industrial waste, including coal waste and fly ash.

Waste like this has a high level of chemical contamination. The North Sea alone receives over ten tonnes of mercury, twelve tonnes of cadmium, 1250 tonnes of lead and 200 tonnes of copper each year.

The effects of marine pollution are often lethal for fish, plants and wildlife, and sometimes they are lethal for humans too. Marine debris – such as plastic – kills some two million sea birds a year as they eat it or become entangled in it. Eventually, most of it ends up as ugly litter on the beaches. Oil pollution not only kills sea birds and spots the sand and shingle with tar, but leaves a poisonous residue of the chemicals in the water which can destroy animals and plants.

Thousands of chemicals, like mercury (from the pulp and paper industry), lead from petrol (which damages children's brains), and pesticides, are released into the sea, causing fish diseases and the disappearance of species. In low concentrations these chemicals may not be harmful, but as they are concentrated in the food chain they can become lethal (as bigger creatures eat smaller ones the chemicals become concentrated). According to *The Good Beach Guide*, forty-six people died and 2,000 suffered crippling mental and physical deformities after eating shellfish from Minamata Bay in Japan. The shellfish had accumulated methyl mercury which had been released into the bay from a local factory.

Sewage is also harmful to human health. It contains bacteria and viruses that can cause a range of infections from upset stomachs to sore throats. And in the past few years we have seen the deaths of thousands of common seals, huge blooms of algae and the deaths and failure to breed of sea-bird colonies in the Orkneys and Shetlands. We don't yet know exactly why these things happen – but it's obvious that the pollution has to stop.

> 'People and companies that pollute the sea and shore are criminals, offending by intent and neglect. Don't let anyone get away with it – the more we remain silent, the worse it will become.'
>
> From *The Good Beach Guide*
> (the Marine Conservation Society).

The European Community has introduced legislation to control pollution but Britain has dodged and prevaricated. In 1989, the Labour Party's Environment Secretary John Cunningham released figures showing that most of Britain's 600 bathing beaches fail to meet EEC standards. Four out of five beaches in the north-west of England and three out of five in the South are not up to EEC standards.

In the same year, the government named 404 designated 'bathing beaches' in line with the EC's Bathing Waters Quality Directive. (The government has chosen to base its judgements on two criteria: the levels of 'total coliform' bacteria and of 'faecal coliform' bacteria which give a good indication of the level of human sewage in the water.) But the Marine Conservation Society say they have more than three times this many 'bathing beaches' on record which don't meet the designated standards.

CLEAN UP ACTION

But there are hopeful signs of improvement. According to the Marine Conservation Society, governments are beginning to realize that the sea is not an infinite dustbin, international agreements are being reached and industry is beginning to clean up its act. They say that this is largely because of pressure from the public. So, if you notice pollution at the seashore, report it to:

- the local water authority
- the environmental health department
- the local council
- the local MP
- the Marine Conservation Society at 9 Gloucester Road, Ross-on-Wye HR9 5BU.

Before you set out on your jaunt to the seaside, check the standards of local beaches with the local tourist office. Or consult *The Good Beach Guide*, published by the Marine Conservation Society. If the beach has been awarded a 'Blue Flag' it qualifies as a relatively clean and unpolluted beach. The Blue Flag awards are organized by the Tidy Britain Group, and they go to beaches:

- with a high standard of water quality
- which are cleaned daily during the bathing season
- which have good facilities: toilets, lifesaving equipment, first aid etc
- where domestic aminals are strictly controlled and driving on the beach is banned.

In 1989, twenty-one British beaches qualified for the Blue Flag.

Lots of dogs and small children together on a limited stretch of sand inevitably mean health risks from dog dirt. Many local authorities are now keeping selected beaches as dog-free zones. Ask the local tourist office – or local people – for information.

Follow the Seashore Code:

- Show respect for sea creatures
- Take your rubbish home with you
- Take photos, not living animals
- Drive on roads, not beaches
- Be careful near cliffs
- Avoid disturbing wildlife.

Or, 'Take nothing but pictures, waste nothing but time, leave nothing but footprints.'

CANCER OF CIVILIZATION

Cancer kills up to a quarter of all people in the West, and the rates seem to be going up. And while cancer is not a particular killer of the young, it is in childhood and baby-hood – and even *in utero* – that many cancers have their genesis. Children who are subjected to radiation or who consume certain pesticides (like the chemical alar, now banned from use in America) may later develop cancers as a consequence.

Finding the 'cure' for cancer has become the Holy Grail of modern medicine, which already responds to the disease with a barrage of drugs, surgery and radiation treatments. But the emphasis has shifted in recent years, with more attention being paid to the 'whole' person. In some treatment centres, like the Bristol Cancer Help Centre, a whole range of techniques, from meditation to counselling and vegetarianism, are used to give sufferers more control over their lives and therefore their cancers.

More recently, the environmental causes of cancer have been coming under scrutiny. It is arguable that cancer as we experience it in the West is one of the penalties of our industrial society. To tackle it we need not only to stop smoking and improve our diet, but we need to look at how we use chemicals in everything from agriculture to food flavouring and cleaning fluid.

Since 1940, the production of synthetic chemicals has increased 200 times. Toxic chemicals get into our food and water from many different sources: they are pumped into the air from industrial chimneys, leaked into water from waste dumps, and sprayed onto food as pesticide.

The latest thinking is that cancer (which is actually some 200 related diseases) develops as a slow process of poison-ing from a wide variety of sources. Smoking is blamed for 30 per cent of cancers, while general environmental causes

'The evidence linking cancer with the industrial environment was further strengthened when researchers started to "map" the disease. Concentrations of cancer were discovered cheek-by-jowl with petrochemical factories ... Mapping has also revealed "clusters" of cancers around chemical factories, nuclear reactors, refineries and in farming areas where there is heavy pesticide use.'

New Internationalist, August 1989.

are thought to be at the root of 10 to 15 per cent. Again, estimates vary, but up to a third of all cancers may be related to diet (see Food).

Radiation from the most 'natural' source, the sun, is now known to cause skin cancers, and major campaigns are underway in countries like Australia to get sun worshippers to cover up. Babies and young children, especially those with fair skins, are susceptible to damage from the sun's rays, even when the sun doesn't seem to be very strong.

KEEPING HEALTHY

As the balance shifts away from western medicine, with its emphasis on curing symptoms, towards a more complete view of health care, traditional ways of keeping healthy are gaining credence again.

- Try to maintain a healthy and balanced diet. Children especially need the right balance of nutrients, and must be protected from 'unhealthy' food for the sake of their present and future health. Alas, much of modern food is contaminated with pesticide residues and further degraded by heavy processing (see Food). Feed your family home-grown or organic food wherever possible, and cut down on your consumption of meat and dairy products.

- Take plenty of exercise. According to Friends of the Earth, only one in five of modern children gets enough exercise and there is growing concern that we are raising a generation of hopelessly unfit youngsters. Physical fitness guards against disease and helps maintain mental well-being, while exercise offers release from stress. So unplug that television and urge the children outside to play. Or take them cycling, swimming and walking.
- Guard against environmental hazards – like pollution. Our air, our water and our land is increasingly polluted with the chemicals and toxic wastes of modern society. As much as possible, keep children away from environments that you suspect of being unhealthy – like polluted beaches and congested streets. Avoid sources of pollution in your home too, like cigarette smoke, chemical cleaners and DIY products (see Home). Unfortunately we can't all afford to live in the healthiest environments, and the clear links between poverty and ill health persist in the West as they do in the Third World.

PREGNANT PAUSES

It is a fact long recognized by animal breeders that the good health of both the male and the female parent – before conception – is crucial to the health of their off-

'If the baby is battling infection or anti-
bodies, has not enough of the substances he
needs or too much of the substances which
are harmful to him, he is at a disadvantage
. . . Foresight believes that if, prior to conception we can help both parents to be free
from infection or allergic illness; to be eating
a diet (or supplementing their diet) to provide the baby with all the minerals, vitamins
and essential fatty acids needed; to be free
from toxic substances such as insecticides,
artificial food colourings, steroids, nicotine,
alcohol, drugs and toxic metals such as lead,
aluminium etc., then this tragic toll [of ill
health] can be very greatly reduced. Our
results so far confirm this.'

From *Guidelines for Future Parents*
by Foresight.

spring. Yet apart from warnings to pregnant women about
the dangers of smoking and alcohol in pregnancy, the
same biological lessons are rarely applied to people.

Only recently has the idea of 'pre-conceptual care' been
gaining ground. That means being in a good state of
health *before* trying to conceive a child. We now know
that smoking, alcohol, environmental pollution and a
poor diet can leave would-be-parents in a sadly depleted
state of health, short of essential vitamins and minerals
and possibly burdened by toxins. Just as in the animal
kingdom, a range of health problems can result – from
miscarriage and stillbirth to mental retardation and physical disabilities in the child.

We all know of children – or have children – who suffer

from hyperactivity, learning difficulties or allergies (which can cause eczema, asthma, hay fever, headaches and other problems). Foresight, the organisation for pre-conceptual care, say that many children with these problems were born prematurely, were small babies or had feeding difficulties. They believe that pre-conceptual care could prevent many of these health problems. And that means a healthy diet – among other things.

We may be an affluent society, but that doesn't mean we are well nourished (see Food). Food processing destroys or removes some of the essential nutrients of many foods. Food grown on unhealthy soil – depleted by factory farming methods and heavily treated by artificial fertilizers – is unlikely to be healthy food. Highly-refined convenience foods – full of sugar and white flour – actually rob our bodies of the vitamins and minerals needed to metabolize them.

A whole range of chemicals and heavy metals, from polluted air and water to pesticides and food additives could be interfering with our health and reproduction. 'Social poisons', like the contraceptive pill, the coil, alcohol and smoking, deplete the body's reserves of minerals and vitamins. Insecticides may also destroy the essential vitamin choline, while food additives can further deplete the body of vital minerals.

Lead (from leaded water pipes and leaded petrol), as well as cadmium (from industrial pollution and cigarette smoke) and aluminium (from a variety of sources, including cooking pots, drinking water and foil food containers) can be detected, and all three interfere with the body's use of essential minerals.

Mercury is another source of pollution. Fortunately most dentists have stopped doing fillings in children's milk teeth (these teeth soon fall out), but many pregnant women go to the dentist in pregnancy when treatment is free. The foetus is very vulnerable to damage from heavy metals, and mercury is detectable in the urine for several days after the fillings are put in.

Zinc deficiency (caused by the pill, the copper coil, pesticide residues, sugar, alcohol and more) and magnesium deficiency (from fluoride in water) are amongst the other warning signs for parents who want to conceive a healthy child. And pesticides are thought to be the cause of allergy in children.

Foresight offers a lot of information about pre-conceptual care and a range of publications, including *Planning For a Healthy Baby*, giving advice on diet, the 'social poisons' and details of their analysis procedures. For further details send a stamped addressed envelope to the Secretary, Foresight, The Old Vicarage, Church Lane, Witley, Near Godalming, Surrey GU8 5PN.

NUCLEAR POWER: NOT SO GOOD FOR CHILDREN

'The evidence of a raised incidence of leukaemia near Dounreay, taken in conjunction with that relating to the area around Sellafield, tends to support the hypothesis that some feature of the nuclear plants we have examined leads to an increased risk of leukaemia in young people living in the vicinity of these plants.'

From the second COMARE report.

Are nuclear power stations responsible for increasing childhood leukaemia? A lot of experts say 'probably – but we don't yet know exactly how'. What we do know is that radiation is the only known cause of childhood leukaemia. And we have known for some years that leukaemia 'clusters' do occur around nuclear installations.

This phenomenon was examined in 1984 when the first COMARE (Committee on the Medical Aspects of Radiation) group of eminent scientists was set up under Sir Douglas Black. So far there have been three COMARE reports, and they have concluded that the higher rates of childhood leukaemia near nuclear installations are due to more than chance. The burden of proof has been placed squarely on the nuclear industry: childhood leukaemia is assumed to be connected with nuclear plants until they can prove otherwise.

The third COMARE report went so far as to suggest that children living within ten kilometres of the Atomic Weapons Research Establishment at Aldermaston and the Royal Ordinance Factory at Burghfield, Berkshire, run an extra risk of between 30 and 40 per cent of developing leukaemia.

In 1990 new evidence linked childhood leukaemias to high doses of radiation in fathers at Sellafield Nuclear Processing Plant, as a result of possible chromosome damage in their sperm; and studies are now underway to find out if workers in other industries, where radiation levels can also be high, can pass on health effects to their children.

What can you do about the risks? You have to weigh up the pros and cons of living close to a nuclear installation. And get involved in your local anti-nuclear campaign.

NUCLEAR POLLUTION

Since the catastrophe at Chernobyl, some people have carried on arguing that nuclear power is environmentally safe and sound. But most of them work for the nuclear industry.

Usually, nuclear power is only responsible for a tiny percentage of all radiation (about 0·1 per cent). But after a nuclear accident, vast amounts of radioactivity are released with the potential to cause cancers and congenital defects.

Three years after Chernobyl, Soviet villages over a hundred kilometres from the plant were still being evacuated, and the once fertile land around them must be abandoned for many years to come. Animals in the contaminated areas gave birth to badly-deformed young, while strange mutations of plant life showed how radiation can distort the long-established patterns of nature. Estimates of future cancer deaths as a result of the accident vary enormously, but there could be between 5,000 and 100,000 deaths over the next forty years.

The more immediate effects of Chernobyl were felt across Europe too. In Germany, one study showed that nine months after the accident, there was a sudden increase in the numbers of babies born suffering from Down's Syndrome. Radiation took only eleven days to reach the east coast of the USA. In Britain, some sheep farms are still subject to government restrictions as a result of contamination of pastures from the disaster.

PROTECTING YOUR FAMILY AFTER A NUCLEAR ACCIDENT

After Chernobyl, public confidence in official versions of the truth about radioactive contamination was severely dented. People who wanted information about health risks were fobbed off with bland reassurances, and many simply couldn't get through to government offices on the telephone. Short of acquiring your own geiger counter (an expensive and dispiriting measure), there are a range of practical steps you can take to safeguard your family if you think a nuclear 'plume' (a cloud of radioactive pollution) is coming your way.

Peter Bunyard, co-editor of *The Ecologist* magazine and long time environmental campaigner, has written a highly detailed book called *Health Guide for the Nuclear Age* (which is published by Papermac). If you want chapter and verse on the complex radiological implications of nuclear disasters, the effects of the various kinds of contamination on the various kinds of food, this is the book for you.

Otherwise, here are some of the practical measures to protect against contamination, as suggested by Bunyard and others. A good rule of thumb is that a nuclear plume plus rainfall equals trouble. Fallout after an accident can be very erratic, varying by as much as a factor of ten even over short distances. The weather conditions are crucial in determining where 'hot spots' of radiation will fall, and it is rain which bring contamination speedily from the sky to the ground. Therefore:

- Do not drink fresh rainwater.
- Stay out of rain.
- Do not swim in open pools.

If the plume is passing your way:

- Stay indoors as much as possible, and keep children indoors, away from sandpits and play areas. Bigger, concrete-built buildings will be safer than less-substantial, wooden buildings.
- Use reliable contraception: this is not the time to get pregnant as even relatively small doses of radiation in early pregnancy can increase risks of later cancer in the child.

- Do continue with breastfeeding.
- Bring in all washing from the line.
- Shut all windows.
- Switch off ventilation.
- Cover fireplaces.
- Bring pets in from outdoors.
- Put away any loose fittings like curtains and rugs so that they don't gather contaminated dust.
- Bath or shower at least once a day.
- Cover your vegetable garden with plastic sheeting.
- Wash clothes and bed linen every day.
- If you have to go outside, wear waterproof clothing, putting a damp cloth over your nose and throat.

'After the Chernobyl accident, outdoor sand-boxes of kindergartens in the Munich area showed average contamination levels that at nearly 50,000 becquerels per square metre were some forty times higher than previously.'

Peter Bunyard in *Health Guide for the Nuclear Age* (Papermac).

CHOOSING FOOD AFTER A NUCLEAR ACCIDENT

As the results of Chernobyl have so tragically demonstrated, radioactivity can render huge areas of agricultural land and all the food growing there quite useless. In general, upland areas tend to become more polluted, together with poorer soils.

To minimize the risks to your family, don't eat locally-grown food if you suspect your locality has been contaminated. Eat food from the freezer or canned food for as long as you can. Drink bottled water if possible. It is well known by now that the grazing animals like cattle, sheep and goats consume radioactive fallout as they feed over large areas. This radioactivity is then concentrated in their milk and gets into butter, cheese, cream and yoghurt.

Bunyard recommends:

- avoiding all dairy products for forty days
- avoid the meat of grazing animals, but especially game animals.

Honey is also suspect after a nuclear accident as bees can accumulate radioactive fallout by collecting pollen and nectar from flowers. Herbs and wild mushrooms are also to be avoided as these concentrate fallout. In a 'Tomorrow's World' documentary about the aftermath of Chernobyl (14 November, 1989), a cattle herder who lived in one of the outlying villages was found to have the highest level of contamination in his whole community. He admitted to breaking government rules and eating wild mushrooms from the fields.

Similarly, broadleaved plants like cabbages and lettuces accumulate more fallout than others – such as root crops like carrots. Washing and cooking them won't help. Avoid vegetables for several months after fallout. Fish also take in radioactive substances as these are washed into rivers and lakes.

6

Transport

DANGER: CHILDREN ON THE ROAD

Parents have a lot to be concerned about when it comes to modern transport. The immediate safety of our children is a daily worry, quite apart from the poisonous fumes and lead which can damage their health in the long term. Whenever they are late home from school, a friend's house – or anywhere – the spectre of some ghastly traffic accident is hard to suppress.

Britain's safety record for children is amongst the worst in Europe. Almost every day a child dies on our roads. In 1986, 407 children were killed in traffic accidents. Two-thirds of them were walking, a sixth were on bikes. According to the Pedestrians' Association, the rate of death and serious injury for ten to fourteen year olds has more than doubled in thirty years. Traffic deaths account for a quarter of all deaths amongst children between the ages of five and fourteen.

'Why should ten times as many six- to nine-year-old pedestrians per 100,000 population be killed in Scotland as in Sweden? Why should three times as many child pedestrians aged ten to fourteen be killed in England as in Italy? Why should the rate of casualties among fifteen to nineteen-year-old pedestrians have doubled over the past generation? I fear the answer must be that we don't care.

Adam Raphael in the *Observer*,
5 November 1989.

Who is to blame for this carnage, and what can we do about it when our society revolves so blithely around the wheels of the car? So entrenched has our car habit become that we behave as if roads and their traffic have some kind of natural right to cut through our communities, past our schools, shops and houses – and at lethal speeds. All too often we assume that if children are involved in road accidents – while it's sad – they *shouldn't* get in the way. And that ultimately, it's parents who ought to make sure that children don't get in the way – by keeping them indoors, if necessary.

But do we really believe that the freedom of car owners should come before the freedom of the majority – chiefly women and children – who don't have cars? According to Friends of the Earth, who run a major campaign called Cities For People, it is time to challenge the tyranny of motor transport. They say the days of blaming children for traffic accidents should now be over; new studies into the physiology and psychology of children show that children can't be held responsible.

'Children are small. They cannot see or be seen in the streets dominated by parked cars. They have a 30 per cent smaller field of vision than adults. They cannot judge car speeds accurately and have difficulty locating oncoming vehicles by sound alone. They have difficulty paying attention to more than one thing at once, and find it hard to maintain concentration. They are impetuous and frequently have more interesting things to think about than road safety. For all these reasons their ability to cope with traffic is limited.'

From *The Friends of the Earth Guide to Traffic Calming in Residential Areas*.

Now that the experts have confirmed what parents knew all along – that children can't cope alone with road safety – further research studies makes even bleaker reading. Not only are children unable to safeguard themselves from traffic, but most drivers make no attempt to safeguard children either. A study by the Psychology Department of Nottingham University found that drivers did not slow down at all when they passed children walking home from school. Yet this is precisely the time when children – tired yet excited – are not concentrating on traffic.

Another study of drivers and how they react to children crossing roads showed that drivers did nothing to avoid possible accidents until they were too close to stop. The lack of anticipation by drivers was total. And there is a clear link between speed and accidents. Children, especially, are far more likely to be killed if a car hits them at over 25 mph. Yet the speed limit in urban areas is still 30 mph.

It is the poorest children who bear the brunt of all this. Children from deprived parts of the community are seven times more likely to be killed in a collision with a motor vehicle than children from the more affluent parts. Connect this with the fact that only a fifth of the poorest households have a car, while 90 per cent of the richest class have a car, and you get a picture of wealthy suburbanites driving into the inner cities and putting the local children at risk.

> 'The car makes more demands and inflicts more damage on our global habitat than any other commodity – but it is, universally, the most desired artifice in the whole history of humanity.'
>
> Ian Breach in the *Guardian*,
> 13 October, 1989.

CURBING THE CAR

One way or another we must find ways to restrain the use of the private car. For so long it has gloried in its sexy image of power, speed and status. But more and more, as public consciousness grows, the car is becoming a symbol of greed, waste and danger.

If we don't accept the wanton killing of our children on the roads there are two alternatives. We could ban our children from the streets: no cycling to school; no playing outside the house. After all, in 1927, the number of children under fifteen killed on the roads was 1,067 – more than double the 1986 total. This looks as if road safety has very much improved, and in many respects it has. But the figures disguise the fact that this gain has been won at the expense of children's freedom. For many children, these days, the strict limits to the world that they are allowed to explore without adult supervision are set by the nearest roads. And when children live in the city, this means they can't visit friends or play outside without an escort.

The other way forward is a much more radical and long-term solution, of the kind promoted by Friends of the Earth in their 'Cities for People' and 'Kids Alive' campaigns. This alternative is to give people – especially children – priority over cars, by adapting our roads, our vehicles and their speed limits to levels we can safely live with.

CITIES FOR PEOPLE

This approach is already being used in Holland and West Germany where 'traffic calming' measures are making streets liveable in once again. Road layouts have been changed, traffic has been re-routed onto main roads, speed limits of under 20 mph are in force, and cycling and walking is being encouraged for all age-groups.

In the Netherlands, the concept of 'living streets' or *Woonerf* became law in 1976, and has since been followed by Germany, Denmark and other cities in France and Sweden. These countries have some residential streets designated as 'play streets' where the speed limits are as low as 8 mph and signs show children playing football in the road. The schemes have cut down on accidents, improved the local environment and have discouraged the use of cars. People – especially children on their way to or from school – are also more likely to cycle.

'Traffic deaths represent two thirds of all accidental deaths and one quarter of all deaths to children between five and fourteen.'

From the Friends of the Earth 'Kids Alive' campaign.

SLOW DOWN

Speed kills. Accidents happen more often and are more serious when cars are going fast. At 34 mph there is a 50 per cent chance that the pedestrian will be killed when hit, but when a car is going more than 40 mph the risk of death increases by 90 per cent.

When an oil crisis brought motorway limits down from 70 mph to 50 mph, accidents dropped by a third.

If you want to campaign in your locality for lower speed limits – or measures to slow traffic down – contact Friends of the Earth for their 'Cities for People' Action Pack at 26–8 Underwood Street, London N1 7JQ. The Friends of the Earth 'Kids Alive' campaign has three main aims:

- To reduce car speeds to 20 mph on residential roads, and even lower around schools and play areas. FoE wants to see speed limits enforced not only by police but by speed bumps, chicanes and similar changes in the road system.
- The introduction of traffic education in schools. Almost every other European country already has a programme to teach children how to use the roads responsibly and unselfishly. FoE also wants to see the creation of a national Pre-school Traffic Safety Club.

- To change the criminal law to make drivers chiefly responsible for accidents involving children in residential streets. It should no longer be any excuse to say 'the child ran out in front of me, there was nothing I could do', argue FoE.

WALK, DON'T WALK . . .

There are a number of things you can do to make your children safer as pedestrians.

- Encourage children of school age (but not younger) to use the Green Cross Code. Road professionals say that the code improves a child's knowledge of road traffic hazards and how to cope with them. Contact the Royal Society for the Prevention of Accidents at Cannon House, The Priory Queensway, Birmingham B4 6BS (tel: 021 200 2461) for more information.
- Teach them to walk carefully along streets, and set them a good example by giving up bad habits of jay-walking.

The Green Cross Code

- First find a safe place to cross, then stop.
- Stand on the pavement near the kerb.
- Look all round for traffic and listen.
- If traffic is coming, let it pass. Look all round again.
- When there is no traffic near, walk straight across the road.
- Keep looking and listening for traffic while you cross.

- If they are out at night – with or without you – make sure they are wearing something bright so that they are visible in car headlights. You can buy reflective stickers or arm bands in bike shops and/or give them a torch to carry.

The Pedestrians' Association reminds walkers that they have these rights:

- A right to walk on a footway
- A right to ask for a footway to walk on
- A right to free and safe passage on the footway
- A right to walk on a pedestrian crossing
- A right to walk in the road – but only when you have to
- A right to complain – to police and your Council when your way is obstructed by badly parked cars, street furniture, holes in the pavement, advertising boards or anything else.

Another useful RoSPA initiative is the Tufty Club for three to seven-year-olds. It was started in 1961 to help teach young children and their parents about safety on the roads, in the home and near water. Three million children have joined the club with its bushy-tailed squirrel as safety emblem, and it offers a wide and colourful range of books, games, jigsaws and other educational materials on the safety theme, developed for use in playgroups, infant schools, nurseries and at home.

Tufty Club parents are encouraged to teach three simple road safety rules:

- Never go out alone
- Always hold an adult's hand when out
- Remember to stop, look and listen before crossing the road with an adult.

TRAFFIC POLLUTION

Parents also have cause for concern about the direct effects of modern transport on our environment. There are some 500 million motor vehicles on the world's roads, all polluting the air and land (through the dumping of old cars and lead pollution along roads) and indirectly causing pollution of the sea every time an oil tanker spills its load.

Our cities, towns – even villages – are now dominated by road traffic. Cars and lorries pour toxic exhaust fumes into the air causing cancer and acid rain. Roads and car parks take up valuable urban land (up to a third of the land in an average city). And the motor industry consumes precious energy and natural resources at an ever more voracious rate.

Heavy lorries are a further alarming, polluting and destructive presence in the small streets of residential areas. As they turn street corners their long bodies often cut across pavements – and woe betide a cyclist with a child on board, or a parent with a buggy who doesn't get out of the way. Their noise can disturb urban life night and day, while lorry traffic can also cause great damage to underground piping systems, such as water, sewers and gas.

The road building lobby argues that the solution to problems of traffic congestion is *more* roads – by-passes, ring roads and new motorways. But environmentalists

Paying the Price

- **Land loss:** roads now permanently cover up some 12 million kilometres in the western industrialized countries alone.
- **Land pollution:** from abandoned old cars.
- **Air pollution:** traffic is a major source of pollution in the air, contributing 80 per cent of the lead, 85 per cent of the carbon monoxide, 45 per cent of nitrogen oxides and 28 per cent of the hydrocarbons which pollute Britain's atmosphere. The results? Acid rain from nitrogen oxides kills lakes and forests across Europe. Lung cancer deaths from exhaust fumes – especially hydrocarbons – are estimated at 3,000 a year in Britain.
- **Oil consumption:** a third of the world's oil goes into fuelling its traffic. And one day, that oil will run out.
- **Noise pollution:** even in 1976 the Noise Advisory Council estimated that six million people in Great Britain lived in homes where traffic noise was above recommended limits. On many city streets it is impossible to carry out a normal conversation, and the constant rumbling of traffic disturbs the sleep of millions.

counter with the view that more roads will simply attract yet more traffic. They say that the building of the M25 around London is an example of how a new road, which is supposed to relieve congestion, almost immediately becomes congested because it releases suppressed demand for car transport.

CUTTING OUT YOUR CAR?

Could you give up your car? If the answer is yes, you have hit upon the simplest solution to one of the most intractable of pollution problems. But don't add to our mountains of waste by just dumping it: sell it or pass it on, unless it is beyond repair, in which case take it to a scrap dealer.

If you feel you must have a car, there are many things you can do to lessen its load on the environment. Chiefly, avoid using it whenever possible. Walk or cycle on shorter

---

'In order to successfully control the car there should be four main principles on which to work. The aim must be to:

- Reduce the amount of traffic in residential roads.
- Reduce the speed of the remaining vehicles.
- Provide special facilities for cyclists.
- Provide special facilities for pedestrians.'

From *How to Control the Car*, Friends of the Earth 'Kids Alive' Campaign.

journeys. For longer journeys, take the bus or train. With special fares and the British Rail Family Rail Card, public transport can be quite cheap when you travel with children – which is some compensation for other problems you face (see below).

If you do need to drive, try to share the journey with others. Many parents already do this successfully by taking it in turns to take and pick up children from school in a 'car pool'.

CUTTING DOWN THE DIRT

'Lead is a poisonous metal which has no function in the body. Exposure to even low levels of lead in the environment can result in anaemia, high blood pressure and damage to the nervous system. Children are particularly at risk. Lead interferes with their production of vitamin D, while recent research has confirmed years of speculation that low-level lead pollution restricts the mental development of young children, even before birth.'

From *Lead Pollution* information sheet, Friends of the Earth.

There is no way that you can make your car harmless to the environment. But you can take a number of steps to cut down on pollution.

- Use unleaded petrol: it's now widely available and cheaper than leaded. If you already have a car which runs on leaded, Campaign For Lead Free Air (CLEAR) say 30 per cent of petrol used in Britain is unleaded. Most of the change has come with new cars but two million older cars have already been adjusted and a further nine million could follow with a minor adjustment which costs up to £30. Leaded petrol is the source of 80 per cent of lead in London's air.

- Buy a second hand car rather than a new one (new cars use up raw materials and add to the numbers on the roads). Choose one with low fuel consumption which runs on unleaded petrol or get it converted if you can.
- Avoid buying diesel-fuelled cars. Diesel vehicles don't use lead in their fuel – but they are now the main source of urban smoke pollution.
- Tune your car regularly so that it doesn't waste fuel.
- Don't drive around with unnecessary loads or unused roofracks: these will increase petrol consumption.
- Radial tyres – rather than cross ply – will cut your petrol usage by up to 8 per cent as they cut down on tyre drag. Also keep tyres properly inflated.
- Drive carefully and slowly. By slowing down from 70 mph to 50 mph you will cut petrol consumption by nearly a third.
- Take any sump oil to a garage: don't pour it down the drain or burn it. And check for oil leaks in your car: all that oil which drips onto the roads can end up polluting the local river.

BUYING A 'GREEN CAR'?

Arguably, 'green car' is a contradiction in terms. But the giant motor industry wants to be seen to be trying to clean up its act, and the various companies are competing in terms of heavily hyped-up new 'clean' technologies.

The change to unleaded fuel, important in cutting down

pollutants, also leads to the next stage of 'catalytic converters' which remove unburned hydrocarbons, carbon monoxide and oxides of nitrogen from exhausts.

According to John Elkington, co-author of the *Green Consumer Guide*, the widest choice of 'cat-cars' comes from West Germany, with Volkswagon in the lead and Audi a strong contender. Austin-Rover, by contrast, has been slower to 'green' its image, says Elkington (*Guardian* 18 February, 1989), while Ford has launched its 'green' Fiesta which, it claims, is the world's first mass-produced environment friendly car. The Fiesta has a lean-burn engine – an alternative 'clean' engine which operates without a catalytic converter.

Contact the A A or R A C, a local garage, the Friends of the Earth transport department or the latest *Green Consumer Guide* for advice on the best 'green' cars around.

METAL BOX MENTALITY

Harder to evaluate – but horribly evident – are the ill effects of the car on the way we live in the world. People who travel everywhere in a metal box – which has its own microclimate, music and even telephone – have fewer links with the world they live in than people who walk or cycle.

Car drivers and passengers don't have the time to notice the details of their local neighbourhood; they don't get the chance to smile or say good morning to neighbours; they don't know what is going on all around them. Instead of walking to the local shop, chatting to the shopkeeper, saying hello to local people, the car takes its passengers to a huge supermarket out of town, where they file along endless rows of produce amongst crowds of strangers. The car fosters the illusion of separateness which has helped bring the human race to such a dangerous environmental pass.

Karen Christensen, in *Home Ecology*, quotes American architects who believe that cars may 'cause the breakdown of society' because of the way in which they keep people apart. She makes the point that people behave in cars in ways they wouldn't dream of behaving if face to face with other people. Somehow that box of steel and glass, and the distance it creates between people, makes it okay to bully and push and shove a way through the streets.

'Children are at the sharp end of policies that threaten to ruin the urban environment for everyone. For too long we have allowed cars to dominate our every move – despite the fact that only half the adult population can drive. The result is that 5,400 people die every year in road accidents, and three hundred thousand are injured . . . Our towns and cities are planned almost exclusively around people in cars. They speed through residential streets, past schools and playgrounds, without a thought for the impact this has on everyday life.'
From Friends of the Earth *Kids Alive* leaflet.

Relationships between people who live in the same neighbourhood are also damaged by too much traffic. In a classic study published by the *AIP* journal in the USA in March 1972, Appleyard and Lintell found that the more traffic on a street, the less contact between people living on that street. On a street with 'light traffic', residents had on average three friends and six acquaintances each. On a street with 'moderate traffic', residents had about one friend and four acquaintances. But on streets with 'heavy traffic' those numbers sank to less than one friend and three acquaintances each.

Facts from Transport 2000:

- Walking still accounts for 39 per cent of all journeys in Britain.
- Public transport operators in Britain are expected to get some three-quarters of their revenue from fares. In contrast, the continental operators get up to three-quarters of their revenue from grants.
- Only one third of the British population can drive – and only a quarter have access to a car whenever they want it.
- In the past decade, the number of the heaviest juggernauts on our roads has quadrupled – yet the load carried has shrunk by one-eighth.

BIKE BONANZA

There aren't many ways of getting around that beat cycling. It's fun, healthy, cheap, quiet, clean and quick. If it weren't for other vehicles on the road (and the occasional canine) it would be just about perfect. And it gives you a kind of freedom to exercise and get out and about that doesn't often crop up in the early years of parenthood.

Most children love cycling – either under their own steam or in a child seat on a parent's bike. Little ones will sleep in their bike seats too. But make sure they are safely strapped in, and invest in good quality 'kiddyseats'. Ask for advice at a good bike shop or contact the Royal Society for the Prevention of Accidents, Cannon House, The Priory Queensway, Birmingham B4 6BS (tel: 021 200 2461).

It's also sensible to wear bright clothing during daytime, while at night you must (by law as well as common sense) have working back and front lights and a red rear reflector. RoSPA also publishes a free guide to bicycle helmets, which could prevent head injuries to children either on their own bikes or in child seats on an adult's bike. (Remember that everyone should take special care in wet weather, when roads are slippery and brakes less reliable.)

STREETWISE KIDS

The traditional way of teaching children about road safety has been through schemes like the National Cycling Proficiency Tests in schools. These have been run by Road Safety Officers, based at local county councils, and since 1947 millions of British children have taken the tests. The proficiency test is being replaced by a new road safety scheme designed to fit in with modern teaching methods and the national curriculum. Instead of learning by rote and being judged by a final test, children will have lessons on real roads and will be assessed at regular intervals during the course, which lasts up to eight hours.

There will also be lessons called 'Streets Ahead', designed to fit in with national curriculum subjects like Science. The new approach will also provide training for parents and set homework in cycle safety. Local Road Safety Officers will continue to run the shemes.

RoSPA also runs the National Bike Club for young cyclists and their families, giving them the help they need to stay safe on the road. Membership includes third party insurance while cycling, plus a regular magazine, posters, competitions and so on, and costs £4.50, or £7.50 for family membership.

> 'Walking is an alternative to driving, but for speed as well as economy and exercise, cycling is unrivalled. In several London 'commuter races', the cyclist has beaten the motorist, bus and tube users and the pedestrian.'
>
> From *Motoring and the Environment*, Friends of the Earth.

CLEAN ALTERNATIVE

The environmental benefits of cycling are pretty convincing. According to Friends of the Earth, three-quarters of all journeys are under five miles long – easily cyclable (as long as you don't have too many children and/or too much shopping in tow). If more people used bikes, pollution and congestion in cities could be cut down significantly. And if only one in ten commuters would forsake their cars for a bike on journeys under ten miles, fourteen million barrels of oil would be saved each year.

The good news is that we are in the middle of a cycling boom. In the last decade the number of people owning a bike has gone up by a third. There are now some fourteen

'Congested roads, uncaring motorists, un-
sympathetic planners – as a cyclist you've
seen this all too often. You can cycle 1,600
miles on the energy equivalent of a gallon of
petrol and fit sixteen cycles into the space of a
single car, but it takes a concerted effort by
the cycling lobby to ensure that conditions
get better, not worse.'
                    From the Cyclists' Touring Club.

million bikes in Britain. While a lot of people can't drive,
most people can ride a bike.

Tragically, the accident figures are high too. In 1987,
over 5,000 cyclists were killed or seriously injured, and
nearly half of them were school children.

It takes cash and political will to make cycling safer.
Germany has done it with their 'Bicycle Friendly Towns'
project, which means making bike lanes, areas for bikes to
wait ahead of traffic, information offices and rental
centres, and Friends of the Earth are campaigning for
similar initiatives here. Cycle lanes and bike parks are a
feature of most British towns and cities but there are far
fewer than in other European countries (although the
quality of what there is is very good).

TRANSPORT FOR ALL?

Last but not least, parents are concerned as consumers of
transport. Whether it's short trips to school and shops, or
longer journeys to visit friends and family, public transport is often a nightmare for parents and children alike.
When it's available and affordable that is.

Surely, we are just the people that public transport should be designed for. It is still the norm that mothers stay at home with their pre-school children. Yet only a third of British women drive (as opposed to two-thirds of men), and so buses and trains are a must for young families. Practically every aspect of public transport – from the long staircases and escalators (no buggies allowed) to the automated ticket barriers on the London Underground (they snap together at just the height of a toddler's head) – spell trouble for parents.

Babies can't quell hunger to suit a bus or train time-table. Yet breastfeeding a baby on British trains, buses or coaches is reserved for women strong enough to ignore the popular view that this is 'rude' behaviour. As for nappy changing, the sheer physical difficulties are as off-putting as the disapproving looks. In the absence of proper facilities, mothers have no option but to deal with dirty bottoms on the seats, tables or floors of their bus or train. (If you should be faced with this problem, try heading for the first-class compartment – there's lots more room. People may object but you can always move on.)

Older children too are often disapproved of on public transport because they find it hard to sit still for any length of time, and they will rarely maintain an adult-style silence. It's up to adults to become more broad-minded, because children will never change.

TURN FOR THE WORSE

What we need then, is a vastly improved system of public transport – and more of it. Alas, very considerable powers have undertaken to massively expand road transport in the future while the decline of public transport continues unchecked. The Department of Transport estimates a minimum growth in traffic of 83 per cent by the year 2025 – and a maximum of 142 per cent.

But where are all these extra vehicles and their roads to go? By 1989, 110 Sites of Special Scientific Interest in Britain had been damaged by road construction; and seven more SSSIs as well as three Areas of Outstanding Natural Beauty threatened. It's not just the green fields, flowers and wildlife that have to make way for the roads. Road building materials have to be quarried and transported at considerable environmental cost. And then shops and warehouses move out to follow the new roads – leaving town centres to decay.

> 'Over the next thirty-five years, according to the Department [of Transport], traffic levels may increase by as much as two-and-a-half times present levels. Growth on such a scale will almost inevitably result in more deaths and injuries and the further intimidation of non-motorized travellers.'
> From the *Guardian*, 23 August, 1989.

Meanwhile the road construction and motor manufacturing lobby remains one of the most powerful special interest groups in Europe, influencing civil servants and politicans alike. According to journalist Ian Breach, whose 'Can you give up your car?' articles in the *Guardian* provoked strong public response in 1989, 'the Department of Transport has been regarded by many environmentalists for years as an arm of the road building business'.

And the 'company car' system perpetuates the whole

polluting business. Three-quarters of the cars driving into central London in the morning rush hour have some kind of company support say Friends of the Earth.

> 'The financial problem [of company cars] is that the worth of the car and of its use is hopelessly under-valued for tax purposes. Calculations suggest that the shortfalls are £1,000 million and £700 million respectively. So we have a £1·7 billion subsidy to promote car use for the wealthy at the same time as the government progressively cuts back financial support for our train and bus services.'
>
> From 'Cities for People' action pack, Friends of the Earth.

Can we put our faith in any of the chief political contenders when it comes to the radical changes needed to break the tyranny of the car? The Conservative commitment to private rather than public transport belies the 'green' image they have tried to cultivate. The Labour Party is keen to revive public transport, but is so far reluctant to curb car-users. So are we going to continue driving down this road until pollution of water, land and air threatens our health and that of our children irrevocably? Until we run out of oil and the raw materials which the motor industry so ruthlessly gobbles up? Or are we going to start now to change the travelling habits of a generation – before the next one condemns us for our folly?

GROUPS AND ORGANIZATIONS

If you want to do something positive about transport beyond the level of personal choice, why not contact or join one of the groups which are active on this front?

- Chief amongst them is Friends of the Earth which campaigns to reduce traffic, for stronger controls over vehicle pollution, and for better public transport. They produce a range of information leaflets, books and campaigning materials. Their 'Kids Alive' information pack and leaflet on traffic calming are particularly useful. Send a stamped addressed envelope to 26–8 Underwood Street, London N1 7JQ.
- Transport 2000 calls itself the national environmental transport campaign. Backed by British Rail, trade unions and a range of environmental groups, it lobbies central and local government for changes in national transport policies. Transport 2000 wants to see protection of resources – in terms of lives, energy and environment – together with a decent public transport system. Their newsletter *Transport Retort* is quite technical, but carries interesting items. They can be contacted at Walkden House, 10 Melton Street, London NW1 2EJ (tel: 071 388 8386).
- There are fifty-five million pedestrians in Britain, and less than half of us drive a car. This is the starting point of the Pedestrians' Association which campaigns to make roads safer for all – but especially for walkers. They see children's experience as an object lesson in what is really happening on our roads. More and more adults and small children are avoiding the dangers to pedestrians by joining the ranks of the car-users, they say. Yet older children – who can't yet drive but want to get about independently – are more

at risk than ever. The death and serious injury rate among pedestrians in the ten to fourteen age-group has more than doubled in the past thirty years, say the PA: 'their plight is thus a reliable indication of what the overall casualty trend would be if other age-groups did not travel so much by car'.

The PA lobbies in Whitehall, publishes the magazine *Walk* and a range of information leaflets, and advises on local road safety problems. Contact the Pedestrians' Association, 1 Wandsworth Road, London SW8 2XX (tel: 071 735 3270).

'One in fifty of today's school-leavers will be killed or seriously injured [in road traffic] during the next ten years if present trends continue.'
From *You're In The Walking Majority*,
the Pedestrians' Association.

- The Royal Society for the Prevention of Accidents provides a wide range of activities including road safety education for children with the Tufty Club and safe transport campaigns. *Care on the Road* is the RoSPA's monthly newspaper and it also produces the *Safety Education* quarterly for distribution to schools across the country. Contact the Society at Cannon House, The Priory Queensway, Birmingham B4 6BS (tel: 021 200 2461).
- The Cyclists' Touring Club has been promoting cycling and protecting cyclists' interests for over a century. Membership is not cheap at £18.50 a head,

but there is a family membership rate (£30 per household) and half price membership for anyone under twenty-one. And the CTC does have a wide range of benefits for members including: a bimonthly magazine; the CTC Handbook which includes recommended repairers, good bed and breakfasts, travel information and advice on cycling off the beaten track; a cycling advisory service with maps, guides and information; cycling holidays and rallies; and much more. They also offer free legal aid and third party insurance.

The CTC is also actively campaigning for improved cycling conditions, lobbying government and local authorities, negotiating with British Rail over bike facilities on trains and monitoring road 'improvement' schemes to make sure cyclists aren't forgotten. For more details, get in touch with the Cyclists' Touring Club, Cotterell House, 69 Meadrow, Godalming, Surrey.

7

In the Countryside

* rural change * threats to the countryside
* protecting the environment * animal suffering
* life in the country * just visiting
* showing farms to children *

The idyll of the countryside: apple-cheeked children romping carefree through flower-filled meadows, paddling in crystal clear streams, surrounded by a rich and abundant wildlife. . .

Did it ever really exist? Or is this childhood countryside of eternal sunshine just a sentimental trick of memory? Certainly, for country dwellers of the past, life was often hard and poor.

Yet without romanticizing earlier times it is fair to say that the years since the Second World War have seen a dizzying rate of change in the countryside. In a swift and sweeping agricultural revolution, the British countryside has altered beyond recognition. And, without question, there are more drastic changes ahead. These changes have profound implications for the countryside most of us hope our children will still be able to enjoy in years to come.

RURAL REVOLUTION

After 1945, Britain's government decided that never again should this island be made vulnerable by its reliance on other nations for much of its food supply. The post-war imperative became self-sufficiency in food. Farming was set to expand, agriculture was to become more efficient and more profitable. Bigger would be better . . .

But agricultural progress has been destroying the countryside ever since. The drive to grow more and more food has brought huge environmental problems as wildlife and its habitats have been destroyed, landscapes ruined, water polluted and soil eroded. Chemical residues in food – which are especially dangerous to children – can now be found in almost all fruit and vegetables grown in this country.

> 'There is not the slightest chance of achieving a healthy countryside if the prevalent utilitarian view, which holds that resources have no value unless they generate wealth, continues to be favoured by those in power . . . The policies which determine the fate of Britain's countryside today are narrow in outlook and based on short-term expediency and greed.'
>
> The 1989 Committee of Environmentalists in their manifesto *The Countryside We Want*.

Steadily, the larger specialist farms have absorbed the smaller more varied ones. Wealthier farmers have prospered as never before: smaller farmers have gone out of business. Big machines have taken over from human labourers until the farming workforce has been reduced to a third of its pre-war size. Chemical fertilizers and pesticides have replaced the age-old systems of crop rotation and animal manure. The modern, computer-run phenomenon of agribusiness has all but taken over.

This is a very British phenomenon. On average, British farms are much bigger than those in the rest of Europe. Even in the past decades, Britain has changed from an importer to a major exporter of cereals. This overproduction is so serious that to control it, several million hectares of land may have to be taken out of farm production.

> 'Over the last ten years or so, the media image of the farmer has changed dramatically: he's no longer portrayed as a bucolic, straw-sucking yeoman, but as a crafty businessman raking in government subsidies and producing mountains of food that nobody wants.'
> Charlie Pye-Smith, ecologist and author.

The more that farmers have been able to concentrate on growing cereals – with the help of new technologies, pesticides and a tenfold increase in artificial fertilizers since 1950 – the less varied and interesting our countryside has become. And our production of more and more food and timber has continued with some disastrous implications for Third World countries – not to mention the expensive and wasteful food 'mountains' which loom above Europe. Yet it is government policies which are responsible for leading farmers down this path, and which have allowed building and tourist developments to compound the destruction.

COSTS TO THE ENVIRONMENT

The environmental consequences have been devastating. Since the last war, up to a half of our ancient woodlands have been lost. More than half of our fens have been drained to make way for crops, many of which merely add to an already surplus supply. Heathlands have been lost or fragmented into small pockets of their former glory.

> 'Ancient woodlands, hedges, old meadows, heaths, wetlands are all disappearing at an alarming rate. Without these habitats much of our wildlife faces extinction.'
>
> Friends of the Earth

Hedges are a valuable habitat for animals and plants. But since the Second World War, 140,000 miles of hedgerow have been pulled out. If this rate of destruction continues, thirty plant species – including sweet violet, dogwood and golden rod – could become extinct in many parts of our countryside, and 250 other plant species will be severely reduced.

As their habitats have been destroyed, so many once common species of animal now face extinction. Otters, once familiar on many British rivers, have all but gone. Birds like the peregrine falcon lost up to half of their numbers in the 1950s and 1960s. The widespread use of pesticides in farming has added to the destruction. According to the RSPB (Royal Society for the Protection of Birds) every wetland important to birdlife in England or Wales is under threat of drainage, or is already being destroyed by piecemeal drainage. A recent report from the House of Lords (*Habitat and Species Protection*, HMSO, August 1989) says that our biologically richest areas are threatened with disaster.

Destroyed since the war:
- 95 per cent of wild flower meadows
- 75 per cent of heaths
- 80 per cent of dry grasslands.

Agriculture now accounts for a fifth of all recorded water pollution incidents. Farm waste, like slurry, is the most rapidly rising source of river pollution, while nitrates from agricultural fertilizers are polluting the drinking water of five million Britons to a level above EEC safety standards.

IMPERFECT PEACE

There is another kind of violation going on in the countryside which particularly affects children – and turns the most peaceable of parents into angry, fist-waving furies. That is the terrifying noise of low-flying warplanes as they scream overhead, sometimes as low as 100 feet.

> 'It's a stroke of luck that no civilians have been killed. But the way things are going, it's only a matter of time before a plane comes down in a built-up area.'
>
> David Steel MP

Hundreds of thousands of holidaymakers who travel to Britain's national parks and scenic areas are finding the rural peace is shattered, while thousands more country dwellers are forced to live with the aircraft noise. It's a problem which has got a lot worse in the last decade and – because of the latest changes in military technology – low flying looks set to become even lower and more intensive.

According to a report in the *Guardian* (2 August, 1989), MPs are receiving a steady stream of protests from anxious parents, schools, hospitals and farmers. And in the estimation of an Edinburgh University academic, 116 aircraft have crashed while hugging the ground, causing 105 deaths. (The RAF does not reveal figures on low-level accidents.) In 1988, two Tornado aircraft collided and exploded above Cumbria, killing four airmen. How long before we face another major disaster?

Address your complaints to the Ministry of Defence (low-flying military aircraft complaints department) DSBc, Main Building, Whitehall, London SW1A 2HB. And write to your MP expressing your concerns.

CHANGE ON THE HORIZON

Terrible though much of the countryside's despoilation has been, there are signs of change on the horizon – and many causes for optimism.

People in Britain are showing real concern about environmental issues, and, together with the Netherlands, this country has the strongest voluntary nature conservation movement in Europe. Three million people belong to Britain's environmental and countryside groups. Visiting the countryside is our most popular national pastime and increasingly – with the backing of major media campaigns – the countryside is being perceived as a very important part of our national heritage. In a 1987 Gallup poll, 70 per cent of the public said they would pay more to the old rate system and in taxes to improve their environment, and would also pay more for food if only the hedgerows and trees could be left intact.

It looks as if the tide of agribusiness is turning. Cereal production may at last be coming down, together with EEC spending. Farmers are now being offered incentives to grow less food per acre and new initiatives are underway to encourage farmers in environmentally-sensitive areas (ESAs) to return to more traditional methods of farming.

In many respects the countryside has reached a crossroads of its own. We now have a golden opportunity to restore much of its abundance and variety. We have a responsibility too: Britain remains the last refuge for many plants and animals which have now vanished from the rest of Europe.

As parents there are many practical and positive things to do – and for our children to do – to help ensure that this opportunity is not a wasted one. Whether you want to get involved with nature activities with your children at home, or join some more structured, national organisations, here are some useful ideas:

Nature in Your Backyard

- Encourage wildlife – and protect your children from chemical hazards – by making your garden a pesticide-free zone. The 'all muck and magic' organic gardening centre, the Henry Doubleday Research Association, has an advice centre plus mail order catalogue to help you deal with pests without poisoning other creatures. Contact HDRA, National Centre for Organic Gardening, Ryton-on-Dunsmore, Coventry CV8 3LG.

- Grow nectar flowers for the insects – such as michaelmas daisy, sweet william, wallflowers, phlox and buddleia (the 'butterfly bush').

- Show the children how to feed birds in winter, and provide a few nest boxes. Birds can be fed many of the scraps from your table – such as bread crumbs, fruit, cheese and bacon scraps, cooked rice and oatmeal. They also like sunflower seeds and wild bird seeds (from pet shops). And provide birds with water for drinking and bathing in too.

- When your children are old enough to be safe near water, dig a shallow pond for frogs.

- Leave a heap of logs and fallen leaves for hedgehogs to hibernate.

- Put the lawn mower away and save some petrol: you've now got good reasons to let part of your lawn grow wild.

Watch Out!

WATCH is the young people's conservation organisation which encourages children to monitor pollution. With 30,000 children as members, plus 8,000 affiliated groups (such as Cubs and Brownies), WATCH is the biggest environmental group for children in the country (see Home, page 12, for more details).

With the help of adult volunteers, the children take part in weekend events like pond dipping, nature rambles, overnight camping and even organized holidays. They can also take part in the WATCH monitoring projects – like the scheme to monitor acid rain. Children were sent kits to monitor the acidity of rainfall in their own streets or gardens and children all over Europe joined in.

There has also been a Watch on stream pollution: children sent in samples from their local stream for analysis. In 1989 WATCH organized their Barn Owl Project with children looking out for barn owl 'windows'.

Members are sent the club magazine *Watchword* three times a year, plus a local newsletter for WATCH groups. Membership costs £3.50 for individuals, or £8.50 for three years. Children can be any age from six to sixteen, although most WATCH members are in the eight to twelve age-group.

Local WATCH groups are run by the Wildlife Trusts (or Trusts for Nature Conservation) in each county, under the national umbrella of the Royal Society for Nature Conservation. For more details, contact the WATCH Trust for Environmental Education, 22 The Green, Nettleham, Lincoln LN2 2NR (tel: 0522 752326).

National Trust

The National Trust – the landowning charity and conservation group (which also happens to be the biggest
private landowner in the country) – has plenty to offer
parents and children, from its 250 historic buildings to
gardens and parks, downlands, lakes, mountains and half
of our finest coastline. It even owns forty traditional villages and hamlets. And many of the wardens at individual
Trust sites have their own 'green activities' organized
especially for children (contact the NT Education office
for details).

The Trust is very keen to encourage children – in the
company of their parents or teachers – to make the most
of their considerable resources. Towards the end of the
1980s, the NT appointed an Education Manager and
began beefing up their education policy. Their aim is to
make sure that children's visits are memorable and enjoyable and that children's questions are encouraged. Children can get involved in 'role-playing' (in historic houses),
'detective work', making or doing things, or guided walks
with Trust staff.

The Trust also wants to provide – eventually at every
property – tangible evidence of a welcome to children in
the form of the Young National Trust newsletter, children's guides, and suitable things to buy in the NT shops.
They are giving special attention to school visits to houses,
and close links are being established with local education
authority curriculum advisers to make sure that what the
Trust has to offer is in line with what schools want and
need. Teachers' packs and schoolrooms are provided at
some properties.

Older junior and secondary schoolchildren can also
enjoy productions by the Young National Trust Theatre.
This is a professional theatre-in-education company run

by the NT which aims to get children thoroughly involved in the 'living history' which its dramas bring to life.

The NT also runs the week-long Acorn Projects for young people over sixteen. These are volunteer working holidays; from about £25 for a week's residential break, enthusiastic youngsters can get down to the soil for plenty of scrub-bashing, rhododendron clearing, footpath maintenance, or even wall-mending for the more experienced. Contact Beryl Sims, The National Trust, PO Box 12, Westbury, Wiltshire BA13 4NA (tel: 0373 826302).

There are special NT membership rates for family groups and for people under twenty-three. Young members also get the lively quarterly, *Young National Trust*, with plenty of ideas and activities. For more information, contact The National Trust, 36 Queen Anne's Gate, London SW1H 9AS (tel: 071 222 9251).

Common Ground

Hundreds of groups – including many schools – have been getting involved in the Parish Maps Project, organized by the environmental charity Common Ground. The idea is to encourage people to chart the things they value. It is local people – and especially children – who know their area intimately, through playing in the parks or woods, through walks and bikes rides, through climbing trees and paddling in streams.

It doesn't have to be a formally drawn map; so far, parish maps have been made in the form of quilts, paintings, photographs, collages, performance and music.

With its focus on culture and locality, Common Ground is behind a range of imaginative projects, including 'Trees, Woods and The Green Man' (expressing our deep feeling for trees), 'The New Milestone Project' (expressing the meaning of place in sculpture) and the 'Save Our

'Make friends with a tree: trees are not fragile ornaments, but tough, enduring, dependable creatures – if we treat them well. They are our friends and we can learn an enormous amount from them. Get to know a tree from day to day, through the seasons, from decade to decade. Climb a tree, lean against it, feel its strength, stability and quietness. Trees have no voice – we must speak up for them.'

From *A Manifesto for Trees* by Common Ground.

Orchards' campaign (to preserve old orchards and plant new ones). For more information about all this and their other schemes, contact them at 45 Shelton Street, London WC2H 9HJ.

Tidy Youth . . .

Improve your area – and have fun! That's the message of the Keep Britain Tidy Group with its Youth Action Pack. It's designed for 'all types of youth group – from the very organized to the very unorganized' particularly with eight to thirteen year olds in mind. The Youth Action Pack has thirty-one sheets of suggestions for a range of activities from organizing a survey to holding an exhibition, making models or playing games and puzzles. They cost £2 each plus postage from The Keep Britain Tidy Group, Bostel House, 37 West Street, Brighton BM1 2RE.

How Now Barn Owl?

The Woodcraft Folk are a kind of a green alternative to cubs and brownies. With 530 local groups bringing boys and girls together for nature-based activities – as well as singing, dancing and so on – they aim to teach children ways of living in co-operation and harmony with nature and with each other. Contact the Woodcraft Folk at 13 Ritherdon Road, London SW17 8QE (tel: 081 672 6031 or 081 767 2457) for details.

For the Birds . . .

Young bird fanciers have their own group – the Young Ornithologists Club – within the Royal Society for the Protection of Birds.

Members can take part in the 'Action for Birds' project which suggests twenty-one practical conservation tasks for young people. The tasks range from creating habitats – like ponds, insect nest sites and bat boxes – to getting other people involved and interested in wildlife through nature trails, poster competitions or conservation displays. Groups taking part in Action for Birds can also qualify for 'Action Awards'. The Action for Birds Project Guide costs 50p. Contact the young ornithologists at YOC, c/o RSPB, The Lodge, Sandy, Bedfordshire SG19 2DL (tel: 0767 680551).

Saving Wildlife

The Young People's Trust for Endangered Species aims to involve children in saving wilderness areas and the rare species which live there. They run field studies courses and publish fact sheets as well as a booklet called *Britain's Rare and Vanishing Species*. Contact YPTES, 19 Quarry Street, Guildford, Surrey GU1 3EH (tel: 0483 39600).

Children who are concerned about wildlife all over the world should join the World Wildlife Fund which has a very active education department with loads of campaigns, publications and projects. They can be contacted at Panda House, Wayside, Godalming, Surrey.

ANIMAL SUFFERING

The fate of our countryside has also had profound consequences for the domesticated animals. As farming has become less diverse and more intensive, hens and pigs have been put into huge factory units. Ninety-six per cent of our hens are now battery farmed. They live four at a time in cages so small that they can never spread their wings or even dust themselves. Stress breeds abnormal behaviour – like cannibalism – in such birds.

According to the Compassion In World Farming group, more than half of British sows are kept throughout their lengthy pregnancies in narrow sow stalls, standing or lying on concrete unable to exercise or turn around – some chained permanently to the floor. The sow then has three weeks with her litter before she is put to the boar again. Sometimes she is lined up with other sows in what is known as a 'rape rack'.

For many cattle too, the days of gentle grazing in the fields are gone. In the 'zero grazing' system, grass is cut and taken indoors to the cattle. Veal calves too are still raised in cruel conditions, kept in narrow crates for half their lives to provide 'white veal' for the consumer.

Cruelty is also rife in abattoirs and in the transporting of live animals. Many lambs and pigs are badly injured after being packed tightly into lorries.

Getting sick of chicken?

- Of the 400 million plus chickens reared in factory farms each year, 25 million die of stress before they are ready for slaughter.
- The corn fed to chickens – together with recycled chicken waste – is grown intensively with the use of pesticides and fertilizers – adding to the pollution of the countryside.
- Factory-farmed chickens are often drugged with antibiotics to fight off the diseases caused by overcrowding.

HUMANE TO ANIMALS

Compassion In World Farming are the foremost group in campaigning against cruel factory farming methods. They have produced a charter for humane rearing of livestock and their schools project, 'The Place of Animals in the Farm', has been circulated to 30,000 schools throughout Britain. To find out more, contact Compassion In World Farming, 20 Lavant Street, Petersfield, Hants GU32 3EW (tel: 0730 64208).

The CIWF Guidelines for Humane Animal Farming are:

- Animals should have freedom of movement and be able to stand up, lie down, and extend their limbs without difficulty; they should not be permanently tethered or confined in stalls or cages.
- They should be able to exercise in a natural way every day.

- Housed animals should have access to clean bedding; free-range animals to clean pasture.
- Animals should have access to clean water at all times.
- Food should be adequate, regular, palatable and suitable, without added drugs or chemicals other than those prescribed by a vet.
- Animals should have shelter from extremes of weather and temperature.
- They should have adequate daylight, and not be subject to excessive artificial light.
- Animals should not be mutilated in any way.
- Transporting of live animals should be reduced as much as possible.
- Slaughtering should be carried out as painlessly as possible.

(In 1986 the Real Meat Company in Warminster became the first British meat producer to adopt the CIWF guidelines.)

PEOPLE IN THE COUNTRYSIDE

Meanwhile, as the countryside changes, many of those who live in the countryside have found themselves increasingly out of work and out on a limb. Post-war planning policies ensured that industry was confined to the towns and cities and most country dwellers now work in the service sector, or they commute to nearby towns. Less than a sixth of those who live and work in the countryside are still employed on farms. And as the new motorways dissected the country, those who could afford it moved out of the crowded suburbs, competing for houses so that local people could no longer afford them.

Many indigenous country dwellers have been left on an

island of unemployment, surrounded by affluent incomers. A quarter of rural households live below the poverty line. Village shops and post offices, doctor's surgeries, schools and bus services have dwindled away or been cut by successive Tory governments. In a survey by the Women's Institute, 54 per cent of villages had no doctor's surgery, 75 per cent had no chemist and 84 per cent had no dentist.

It is women and their children who have been particularly affected by the decline of public services to villages. Nursery provision – already desperately inadequate throughout the country – is ten per cent below average in country areas. Women and children are also the chief customers for public transport, and this has been cut drastically. In 1985 only a third of British women over seventeen could drive a car. Yet our bus services have been cut back more than in any other European country in recent years, while bus fares have gone up and up. The shrinkage of our rail network has implications not only for village dwellers but for townspeople wanting to get to the countryside. In 1963 Britain had some 17,000 miles of rail. By 1983, this total had shrunk by a third. Over two thirds of those visiting the countryside go by car.

VISITING RIGHTS

Yet people do want to get to the countryside. In a 1984 survey by the Countryside Commission, 85 per cent of the public made at least one trip to the countryside for recreation each year.

When the public get there, what they want to do is walk. But virtually all of our countryside is now owned and managed either as farmland or as forestry – and in England and Wales the public are not allowed in.

The battle for freedom of access to the countryside has been going on for over a century. It has seen the mass trespass movement, it has seen a variety of Bills and Acts pass through parliament (not all of these have been entirely progressive: the 1981 Wildlife and Countryside Act made it legal for farmers to keep bulls in fields with public paths!).

Yet much of our countryside is still not open to the public – not even in our national parks or Areas of Outstanding Natural Beauty. And as any keen walker knows only too well, even the designated footpaths which do legally belong to the public have often been blocked or ploughed up by farmers. In a 1984 survey by the Countryside Commission, 60 per cent of paths in arable fields had been 'adversely affected' by farming.

The situation is better in the more remote and upland areas of the country, where sheep and cattle graze on open land. But few families can drive long distances for a serious hike up a mountain; what they need is a walk of a few miles without spending all day in the car to get there. But the land which is closer to towns and cities, especially in the heavily-populated South, is often heavily cultivated and lacking in suitable footpaths.

Public access to woodland is also limited, often by landowners who claim – without much evidence – that walkers will disturb pheasants or partridge intended for a shoot.

Nor is a walk in the country always a healthy affair. Three per cent of arable land is subject to aerial spraying with pesticides, and spray from tractor-pulled booms may dowse walkers with dangerous chemicals. In one case in 1985, according to Friends of the Earth, a group of school children were repeatedly sprayed by an aircraft while they stood waving at it.

Despite the difficulties, most people want to visit the countryside more. The Countryside Commission say that

> 'The freedom on which the countryside's present owners and managers insist is the freedom to deny us access to the land, to deprive us of the rich and variegated landscape we once enjoyed, to rear animals in conditions many of us find abhorrent, to douse fields with chemicals that kill wildlife and pollute drinking water.'
>
> *The Countryside We Want*

going out into the countryside is one of Britain's most popular recreational activities, with 120,000 miles of public footpath, bridleways and byways to choose from, as well as many other areas of moorland, heath, seashore and woodland. Increasingly, access to the countryside – just like life in the villages – is becoming a privilege which only the more affluent can afford. In the Countryside Commission survey (1984), more than half of the richest social class said they go to the countryside 'a lot' compared with only a quarter of the poorest social class.

> 'The withdrawal of bus and rail services and the escalation of fares has done more than the gamekeepers ever did to prevent people getting out into the countryside.'
>
> The Socialist Countryside Group

FOOTLOOSE . . .

The Ramblers' Association works to protect the countryside and fights for more public access. Their programme of organized walks includes more and more groups suitable for parents with young children. They will provide information about renting cottages, ideas for holidays and advice on walking gear; contact the Association at 1–5 Wandsworth Road, London SW8 2XX (tel: 071 582 6878).

THE COUNTRY CODE

Perhaps your children have grown up in the heart of the country, absorbing knowledge and understanding of its ways with their mother's milk. But for the nine out of ten of us who are urban dwellers, we can help our children enjoy and respect the countryside by sticking to the Country Code:

- Leave livestock, crops and machinery alone
- Take your litter home
- Help to keep all water clean
- Protect wildlife, plants and trees
- Take special care on country roads
- Make no unnecessary noise
- Enjoy the countryside and respect its life and work
- Guard against all risk of fire
- Fasten all gates
- Keep your dogs under close control
- Keep to public paths across farmland
- Use gates and stiles to cross fences, hedges and walls.

Countryside Access Charter

Your rights of way are
- Public footpaths – on foot only. *Sometimes way-marked in yellow*
- Bridleways – on foot, horseback and pedal cycle. *Sometimes waymarked in blue*
- Byways (usually old roads), most 'Roads Used as Public Paths' and, of course, public roads – all traffic. *Use maps, signs and waymarks. Ordnance Survey Pathfinder and Landranger maps show most public rights of way.*

On rights of way you can
- Take a pram, pushchair or wheelchair if practicable
- Take a dog (on a lead or under close control)
- Take a short route round an illegal obstruction or remove it sufficiently to get past.

You have a right to go for recreation to
- Public parks and open spaces – on foot
- Most commons near older towns and cities – on foot and sometimes on horseback
- Private land where the owner has a formal agreement with the local authority.

In addition you can *use* by local or established *custom or consent*, but ask for advice if you're unsure
- Many areas of open country like moorland, fell and coastal areas, especially those of the National Trust, and some commons
- Some woods and forests, especially those owned by the Forestry Commission
- Country Parks and picnic sites
- Most beaches
- Canal towpaths
- Some private paths and tracks.

Consent sometimes extends to riding horses and pedal cycles.

FARM VISITS FOR CHILDREN

Fewer and fewer children have the opportunity to grow up on – or near – farms these days. But there are plenty of other ways to give children the chance to see what goes on there.

- Organic farming is the most environmentally-sound way of producing healthy food. It uses methods which co-operate with – instead of dominating – natural systems. There are now about a thousand organic farms operating in Britain. These do not rely on artificial fertilizers for fertility, or poisons for pest control, and so they take a lot of hard work. Hence the WWOOF scheme – Working Weekends on Organic Farms. In exchange for your work (full time and quite hard!) the farmer offers bed, board and transport to and from the local station. Although most 'Wwoofers' tend to be young single people and WWOOF members need to be over sixteen, some farms are prepared to take families with children. For more information, contact WWOOF, Working Weekends on Organic Farms, 19 Bradford Road, Lewes, Sussex BN7 1RB.

- The Commonwork Centre in Kent is based on a 500-acre dairy farm, twenty-five miles from London. With their ideal of making the most of human and environmental resources, they make plant compost from their cattle manure, handmade bricks from waste clay displaced in the construction of the dairy – and so on. Children (mostly in school groups) get the chance to experience a whole range of activities from milking cows to making yoghurt. Commonwork also offers an extraordinary range of educational projects such as making woodburning stoves from clay, making 'homes' from straw, building 'survival' shelters in

the woods or doing a survey of the farm's use of
energy. See 'Education' too. Contact the Commonwork Centre, Bore Place, Chiddingstone, Nr Edenbridge, Kent TN8 7AR.

- *Farms to Visit in Britain* is a booklet which gives a full
  list of farms across the country that are open to visits
  by school parties and the public. There is usually a
  small fee (and a group fee for school parties). These
  farms can provide a golden opportunity for children to
  observe all aspects of farming, from rare breeds to
  milking demonstrations, seasonal lambing, shearing
  or dipping, or even a sheep-dog trial. Make sure that
  children are properly dressed for a farm and that they
  follow the Country Code.

  The booklet was published in British Food and
  Farming Year (1989) by the Shell Education Service
  together with the National Farmers' Union and the
  Association of Agriculture. It is available free from
  these addresses: National Farmers' Union, Farming
  Information Centre, Agriculture House, Knightsbridge, London SW1X 7NJ (the NFU also operates a
  Farming Information Centre to the public from this
  address); the Association of Agriculture, Victoria
  Chambers, 16/20 Stratton Ground, London SW1P
  2HP (the Association also operates a farm visits
  service for groups of school children over thirteen,
  plus teacher training courses in regional centres); or
  Shell Education Service, Shell UK Ltd, Shell-Mex
  House, Strand, London WC2R 0DX (requests from
  teachers only; Shell Education Service also offers a
  free catalogue, *Resources For Teachers*).

- City farms with their sheep, goats, ducks, geese and
  rabbits give children the chance to enjoy domestic
  animals in other than countryside locations. The city
  farm movement began in 1976, providing little urban

oases which exist in often stark contrast to their massive country counterparts where too often profit is persued at the expense of the environment. There are now sixty-six city farms throughout the country using mostly organic methods and providing all kinds of educational opportunities to children and the community.

'There was a visitor [to Elm Farm in south London] who was amazed to find that ducks have legs. She had only ever seen them legless as they moved across the water. There is also a need to show children where food comes from – like the school group which couldn't believe that hens actually produce eggs, and the little boy's question about which were the hot and cold teats on the cow's udder . . .'

From *Everywoman*, May 1989.

The London Countryside Bureau has its own guide to farms in most unlikely settings – from freightliner containers in Highbury to the depths of Dockland. Contact the London Countryside Bureau, 23 Cardross Street, London W6 0DP (tel: 081 741 3404).

Many other major cities have their own farms, like Bristol's Windmill Hill City Farm. Children can see and/or do everything from spinning and weaving to making butter. The farm also helps children with special needs to enjoy the experience with all their senses – stroking the rabbits and smelling the goats. There are pony trap rides and egg incubators as well as an adventure playground and a range of holiday activities for children of all ages – like the four to sevens Club for independent infants and the Young City Farmers (aged seven to twelve). This community project was set up to meet demands of local people that derelict land in the area should be used for their needs. Teachers are invited to talk to the Farm's education staff and to arrange school projects there. Windmill Hill City Farm can be found at 38A Doveton Street, off Philip Street, Bedminster, Bristol BS3 4DU.

Details and locations of city farms all over the country are available from the National Federation of City Farms which can be found at, The Old Vicarage, 66 Frazer Street, Windmill Hill, Bedminster, Bristol (tel: 0272 660663).

- Remember that the zoos of many cities have a 'pets' corner' where children can enjoy contact with small and domestic animals.

- Most counties have their own College of Agriculture, complete with schools liaison or environmental studies unit, catering for the needs of school children. Find out about your county college from the Local Education Authority.

- *Enjoy Your Countryside – walk a farm trail* is a leaflet listing farm trails around the country. It is available from Bayer UK Limited, Agrochem Business Groups, Eastern Way, Bury St Edmonds, Suffolk IP32 7AH.

- Children who are fond of animals will enjoy a visit to one of the Rare Breeds farms. A list of such 'farm parks' is available from The Rare Breeds Survival Trust, 4th Street, National Agricultural Centre, Kenilworth, Warwickshire CV8 2LG (tel: 0203 51141).

- One of the best ways for children to get some 'hands

on' experience of farm life is to take them to a farm
where they can pick their own food – be it strawberries, raspberries or broad beans. The Farm Shop
and Pick Your Own Association has a list of farms to
visit, from Agriculture House, Knightsbridge,
London SW1X 7NJ (tel: 071 235 5077), or look in a
local paper.

- For a historical perspective on life in the countryside
why not take your children to a rural life museum
where they may see replicas of blacksmith and
wheelwright's shops, homes of farm workers, as well
as tools and equipment which have been carefully
preserved. Information on where to go nationally is
available from the Museum of English Rural Life,
University of Reading, Whiteknights, Reading RG2
6AG (tel: 0734 318660).

LONDON'S COUNTRYSIDE

In recent years the countryside around London has been a
bit of a battleground with conflicts between farmers, conservationists, developers and the green-space seeking
public. But there have been positive developments, as
many farmers have decided that growing food is not the
only way to make a living. As a result, the London
Countryside Bureau (with support from the Countryside
Commission) has been able to compile a series of guides
for visits to farms, vineyards, rural museums, city farms,
farm produce and country events within easy reach of
London. These cost £2 for the set (or £2.50 with postage)
from London Countryside Bureau, 23 Cardross Street,
London W6 0DP (tel: 081 741 3404).

London tourist offices will also have details about
parks, wild areas and urban nature reserves throughout
the capital.

Useful addresses

Children's Scrapstore, the Federation of Resource Centres, Greater Manchester Play Resource Unit, Grumpy House, Vaughan Street, West Gorton, Manchester M12 5DU (tel: 061 223 9730).

Common Ground, 45 Shelton Street, London WC2 9HJ.

Compassion In World Farming, 20 Lavant Street, Petersfield, Hampshire GU32 3EW (tel: 0730 64208).

Council for Protection of Rural England, 25–7 Buckingham Palace Road, London SW1W 0PP (tel: 071 976 6433).

Commonwork, Bore Place, Chiddingstone, near Edenbridge, Kent TN8 7AR.

Consumers Against Nuclear Energy, PO Box 697, London NW1 7JG.

Countryside Commission, John Dower House, Crescent Place, Cheltenham, Gloucestershire GL50 3RA.

Cyclists' Touring Club, Cotterell House, 69 Meadrow, Godalming, Surrey.

Education Otherwise, 18 Victoria Park Square, London E2 9BB.

Friends of the Earth, 26–8 Underwood Street, London N1 7JQ (tel: 071 490 1555).

Greenpeace, 30–1 Islington Green, London N1 8XE (tel: 071 354 5100).

Green Party, 10 Station Parade, Balham High Road,

London SW12 9AZ (tel: 081 673 0045). **Scottish Green Party**, 11 Forth Street, Edinburgh EH1 3LE.

Green Teacher, Llys Awel, 22 Heol Pentrerheydn, Machynlleth, Powys SY20 8DN.

Henry Doubleday Research Association, National Centre for Organic Gardening, Ryton-on-Dunsmore, Coventry CV8 3LG.

Human Scale Education, c/o Dame Catherine School, Ticknall, Derbyshire.

Intermediate Technology, Myson House, Railway Terrace, Rugby CV21 3HT.

Keep Britain Tidy Group, Bostel House, 37 West Street, Brighton BN1 2RE.

London Food Commission, 88 Old Street, London EC1V 9AR (tel: 071 253 9513).

Marine Conservation Society, 9 Gloucester Road, Ross-on-Wye HR9 5BU.

National Council for Voluntary Organisations, 26 Bedford Square, London WC1B 3HU (tel: 071 636 4066).

National Federation of City Farms, 66 Frazer Street, Windmill Hill, Bristol (tel: 0272 660663).

Parents for Safe Food, Britannia House, 1–11 Glenthorne Road, London W6 0LF (081 748 9898).

Pedestrians' Association, 1 Wandsworth Road, London SW8 2XX (tel: 071 735 3270).

Play For Life, 31b Ipswich Road, Norwich NR2 2LN (tel: 0603 505947).

Play Matters, 68 Churchway, London NW1 1LT.

Royal Society for Nature Conservation/WATCH, The Green, Nettleham, Lincoln LN2 2NR (tel: 0522 752326).

Royal Society for the Prevention of Accidents (RoSPA), Canon House, The Priory Queensway, Birmingham B4 6BS (tel: 021 200 2461).

Royal Society for the Protection of Birds, The Lodge, Sandy, Bedfordshire SG19 2DL (tel: 0767 680551).

Ramblers' Association, 1–5 Wandsworth Road, London SW8 2XX (tel: 071 582 6878).

SCRAM (the Scottish anti-nuclear campaign), 11 Forth Street, Edinburgh EH1 3LE.

Soil Association, 86–8 Colston Street, Bristol, Avon BS1 5BB (tel: 0272 290661).

Tidy Britain Group, The Pier, Wigan WN3 4EX.

Transport 2000, Walkden House, 10 Melton Street, London NW1 2EJ.

Vegetarian Society, Parkdale, Dunham Road, Altrincham, Cheshire WA14 4QG.

Women's Environmental Network, 287 City Road, London EC1V 1LA (tel; 071 490 2511).

Woodcraft Folk, 13 Ritherdon Road, London SW17 8QE (tel: 081 672 6031 or 081 767 2457).

Woodland Trust, Autumn Park, Dysart Road, Grantham, Lincolnshire NG31 6LL.

Further Reading

Blueprint for a Green Planet by John Seymour and Herbert Girardet (Dorling Kindersley, 1987).

C For Chemicals by Michael Birkin and Brian Price (Green Print, 1989).

Children's Food by Tim Lobstein (Unwin Paperbacks, 1988).

Green Consumer Guide by John Elkington and Julia Hailes (Gollancz, 1988).

Green Pages by John Button (Optima, 1988).

Health Guide for the Nuclear Age by Peter Bunyard (Papermac, 1988).

Holding Your Ground by Angela King and Sue Clifford (Wildwood House, new ed. 1987).

Home Ecology: Making Your World a Better Place by Karen Christensen (Arlington Books, 1989).

How To Be Green by John Button (Century, 1989).

Nitrates: The Threat in Food and Water by Nigel Dudley (Green Print, 1990).

Small is Beautiful by E.F. Schumacher (Abacus, 1971).

Teaching Green by Damian Randle (Green Print, 1989).

The Countryside We Want edited by Chris Hall and Charlie Pye-Smith (Green Books, 1987).

The Good Beach Guide by the Marine Conservation Society.

The Green Alternative by Peter Bunyard and Fern Morgan-Grenville (Methuen, 1987).

The Sanitary Protection Scandal by Allison Costello, Bernadette Vallely and Josa Young (Women's Environmental Network).

Index